MOVING UP

Reginald Tshepo Pheqe

About the Author

Reginald Tshepo Pheqe is a devoted husband, a proud father of two, and a hospitality professional whose journey reflects dedication, perseverance, and transformation. Born and raised in South Africa's North West Province, Reginald's early years were shaped by humble beginnings and a deep respect for hard work and purpose. After completing his schooling, he moved to Johannesburg in the Gauteng Province, where he began his professional career in hospitality.

Starting as a waiter, Reginald's passion, discipline, and curiosity for excellence propelled him through multiple management roles, ultimately leading him to become a respected wine connoisseur and sommelier. His career has been a continuous ascent—driven by a belief that nothing is truly impossible. To him, *impossible* simply reads as *I'm possible.*

Reginald's remarkable journey from the red dust of Pella to the polished corridors of fine dining establishments is a story of resilience, faith, and self-discovery. His debut book, *Moving Up*, is both ingenious and heartfelt—a reflection of his life's path and the lessons he gathered along the way. Through its pages, he invites readers to witness how struggle can become strength and how purpose can be shaped from perseverance.

Today, Reginald continues to expand his horizons, working aboard international cruise ships and exploring the world while refining his craft. His story serves as an inspiring reminder that one's origin does not define one's destination; it only strengthens the journey toward it.

Preface

Moving Up is a story of becoming, of how a barefoot boy from Pella, a small village dusted in the ochre sands of South Africa's North West, grew into a man who learned to walk confidently across marble floors without ever forgetting the ground that first carried him. It is a story that lives between two worlds: one of scarcity and resilience, and another of achievement and quiet introspection.

In these pages, *Reginald Tshepo Pheqe* retraces his life's path with honesty, grace, and unflinching memory. From the dry winds that swept across his childhood to the crisp air-conditioned spaces of five-star lodges where he would one day work, his journey is more than a personal reflection; it is a universal meditation on identity, dignity, and belonging.

As a child, Reginald was taught that life did not owe him fairness. He learned early that joy could be handmade from dust, that hunger could teach patience, and that silence could speak volumes. His grandmother, a figure of immense wisdom and tenderness, instilled in him the understanding that love and resilience were greater currencies than money. Through her lessons and the everyday rituals of survival, he began to dream of meaning and recognition.

Years later, standing in crisp suits and professional circles, he would come to realize that success often arrives with an echo of displacement. No title or salary could fully silence the voice that asked, *"Do you belong?"* The more he achieved, the more he understood that true elevation was not about rising above one's past but integrating it, honoring the child who endured, the family who believed, and the soil that shaped him.

Moving Up speaks to anyone who has ever felt like an outsider in the rooms they've earned their way into. It captures the tension between gratitude and doubt, pride and humility, and the quiet reconciliation of identity that comes when one learns that authenticity is the highest form of arrival. Reginald's reflections unfold not as confessions, but as lessons—whispered reminders that greatness is not inherited, but built, breath by breath, act by act.

This book is also an ode to the ordinary people who taught him extraordinary lessons: the friends who played barefoot games in the heat, the teachers who doubted him, the mentors who challenged him, and the strangers who offered kindness when the world turned cold. Their presence, spoken or silent, is woven through every chapter.

In the end, *Moving Up* is not merely a story of ambition fulfilled; it is a testimony to perseverance, identity, and grace. It reminds readers that success does not erase where we come from; it amplifies it. And that the truest measure of progress is not how far one climbs, but how deeply one remembers.

Through his words, Reginald Tshepo Pheqe invites readers to walk with him—barefoot, grounded, and unafraid of the dust that made them whole.

Table of Contents

Chapter 1: The Impostor in the Mirror

He stood in front of the mirror, adjusting the cuff of his suit. The navy fabric sat neatly against his wrist, a noble and professional material that whispered of class and conferences, of soft-footed concierges and poured crystal glasses. The tie was knotted perfectly, the collar pressed sharp, and the shine on his shoes made the polished floor beneath him look like a second mirror. From the outside, it would have seemed like success had wrapped itself tightly around him. But inside, a turbulence stirred.

Reginald looked at the man in the mirror the way a boy looks through a shop window—longing, unsure, unconvinced it was truly his. And then, without meaning to, he said it aloud:

"Who are you pretending to be?"

The words echoed and bounced within him. They were not new. They had followed him, like dust in a desert wind, since the first time he served wine to a billionaire who asked what vintage went best with oysters. Since the first time he was told, by someone trying to be helpful, that he was "so well-spoken" for someone from his background.

Impostor. Pretender. Counterfeit.

No matter how much success he gathered, a part of him still feared it was rented. That one day, someone would knock and ask for the suit back, the job back, the identity back.

Because beneath that tailored fabric, beneath the perfect etiquette and the smooth introductions, lived a barefoot child from the baked red soil of Pella, a village where dreams came with no guarantees and most ambitions died quietly before they could even be named.

He remembered those nights clearly. The silence of the desert was pregnant with old wind and distant sound. He would sit near the corner of his grandmother's home, just a cracked wall and flickering kerosene light between him and the stars, and gaze at the twinkling horizon. Far away, on a mountain edge, lights would blink—city lights, he was told. But to Reginald, they weren't just lights. They were promises.

"It felt like a lonely wolf in the middle of the bush," he would say later, "seeing a spark of light out of nowhere."

Those lights became symbols of elsewhere, of something more. Of places where people wore shoes every day, where meals weren't guessed but guaranteed, and where men like him didn't have to choose between water and dignity. But now, having arrived in that elsewhere, dressed in its uniform and fluent in its customs, he found himself haunted by a different kind of longing. A longing for what he used to be, for his childhood, for his village.

Impostor syndrome is often described clinically, but for Reginald, it was more visceral. It wasn't just self-doubt; it was the remaining ripples of his life that had never truly felt erased. Success had not cured the ache of origin. If anything, it had amplified it.

He thought of the games he played as a boy—hide and seek among thorn bushes, catching birds, chasing whirlwinds that spun up dust and mystery in equal measure. There had been joy there, deep and uncomplicated. You didn't need money to belong. You just needed breath, bare feet, and a laugh that could fill the dusk.

He thought of his grandmother, her voice like soft, folded linen, steady and worn. She believed in him with a blind certainty that the world rarely mimicked. When the whirlwinds came, she would tell the children to point a knife into the air, a ritual she believed could redirect the chaos. But when the bigger storm came—poverty, loneliness, absence—she had only love to shield them. And that had been enough.

Now, in this mirror, there was no whirlwind and no storm. Just a man who had walked through one. A man who had outrun the dust, but still carried it in his lungs.

He had stood in five-star kitchens and high-end tasting rooms. He had learned to name the scent of soil in a glass of wine, to speak in phrases like "oaky finish" and "notes of cassis." And yet, there were times he still stumbled over his tongue, afraid it would betray the village boy still hidden behind it.

There were moments, too many to count, when he entered rooms full of confidence and exited them full of doubt. When his colleagues praised his work, his mind whispered, *Wait until they find out.*

That voice was old. As old as the first time he walked into school barefoot while others wore shoes. As old as the nights he slept hungry, belly cramping, listening to the frogs and crickets and wondering if that kind of quiet was all he'd ever know.

And yet, it wasn't shame he felt now—not quite. It was awe. That this man in the mirror could have emerged from that child, that somehow, he hadn't disappeared. He had grown, learned, and survived.

He reached for the tie again, straightening it. He wasn't pretending. He was becoming. Becoming someone who holds the past not as proof of his struggle.

Still, the mirror did not lie. It only told both stories.

The barefoot child. And the man who never forgot how it felt to walk without shoes.

That barefoot boy had a name. A heartbeat. A hunger—not just for food, but for more. And he still dwelled in Pella, and slept alongside his grandmother.

The mirror was long behind him now, but its image lingered. As Reginald walked through the crisp marble corridor of the luxury lodge, his gait smooth, shoulders squared, his soul still wandered somewhere else. Somewhere dust-covered. Somewhere bone-dry. Somewhere, birds once soared above jagged trees and children chased the wind for fun, not metaphor. His body was in the present, but his heart had folded back into a sun-cracked memory.

Pella was not just a place or a dry village in Africa. It was a presence. The sky above was a bowl of fire in the day and a spilled inkpot of stars at night. In that village, alarms didn't chime. Roosters did. And old diesel buses growled across the plain like tired beasts, signaling time with their engines.

He remembered it all with nostalgia and clarity that only a man who has survived it can have. The smells came first: smoky wood fires, sun-warmed chicken droppings, and the perfume of dry soil gasping under the first kiss of rain. Pella had its own scent, like old pages and cracked hands.

He remembered his grandmother pointing knives into the sky. Not in anger, not in madness—in belief. Whirlwinds danced across their yard like mischievous spirits, and she believed that steel could bend their path. Reginald, too, believed it as a child. And in Pella, children believed in all things because magic was the only explanation for a world so unpredictable, so loud and quiet all at once. Point the knife, she said. Protect the chickens. Beware the eagle.

The eagle. Always watching. High above, with the patience of a God and the cruelty of a thief. It knew when the whirlwind came, the children would scatter. That was its moment. It would strike. Even the birds in Pella played by the rules of hunger and survival.

The children caught birds sometimes. Reginald, giggling and barefoot, would run with other boys, catching, plucking, and roasting over an open fire. The joy was primal. It wasn't cruelty. It was childhood with teeth.

Play didn't require toys. They had grass, dirt, and each other. They had hide-and-seek, laughter without end, and an understanding that whatever joy they felt today might not be there tomorrow. That made them cling to it tighter. When someone disappeared, no one asked too many questions. That, too, was part of life. Nature gave. Nature took.

Evenings brought rest and stories by the fire. His grandmother's voice was as much part of the village as the wind itself. She would stir the pot with one hand, her good one, while her malformed one rested in her lap, useless but dignified. She spoke of animals that talked, people that flew, spirits that warned. Reginald listened not just with his ears, but with his skin, bone, and memory. Those stories prepared him for something. He didn't know what, though.

Moving Up

Children of Pella were not taught lessons about money, economics, savings, or ambition. They were taught resilience. Walk for water. Fetch firewood. Share what you have. If you have nothing, share laughter. And if even that runs out, share silence. It is, after all, the language of hunger.

Reginald knew the pain of isolation early in his childhood days. Children with coins could buy sweets at school. He couldn't. They laughed together. He stood near, hoping proximity might equal inclusion. It didn't. That was another one of the harsh lessons.

He dreamt of haircuts. That's how small the dreams were. A real haircut. Not the village shears that bit into skin and left behind shame. But a haircut like the boys from the city had when they returned with polished shoes and bread rolls in their lunchboxes. He wanted to be them. For a while. Before he realized he had to be something else.

There was no bedtime or goodnight kisses. The stars signaled sleep. So did exhaustion. And that one old bus—its sound marking time, its engine coughing across the village road like it carried the future in its rusted belly.

He had no idea what a boarding school was. Only that his aunt had been to one, and that made her different than the rest of his family. She asked about his day. She brought sweets. She listened. When she left, the silence returned. That silence knew his name. It became his shadow. And still, he went to school. On foot. Barefoot. Because he was told to. Because something in him said he must.

He walked on. Because the boy from Pella had survived, and in some quiet, indelible way, he had won.

In the soft silence of Pella, joy was handmade—stitched from dust, firewood, and imagination. Reginald, barefoot and bruised, ran through that childhood like a boy chasing wind. His soles toughened by thorny paths, his eyes still carrying dreams with no limits

There were no toys. No money. No bedtime stories from books. But there was life. And life, in that part of the North West, was a kind of alchemy. It turned scarcity into folklore and pain into play. A small stone could become a car. A dry stick, a sword. A feather, a prize from the gods.

Other kids had coins in their closed fists, but Reginald had questions.

And he asked them silently—never out loud. Why did they have bubble gum, and he didn't have any? Why did they rub sweets into their palms, laughing, while he stood off to the side, hands empty, mouth closed? Why did they wear shoes—even if just tattered ones—and he walked barefoot, his skin splitting in the cold?

But the shame never had a place to build a home. His grandmother, the matriarch of their world, never let it settle. She fed them with her hands and her hope. She could simmer a stew from almost nothing and fill their bellies with pride. "She made our shack feel like the warmest place on earth," Reginald remembered. It wasn't just what she gave. It was how she gave it—like her stories beside the fire weren't just entertainment, they were lessons; like the kiss she placed on his forehead after a long day wasn't routine, but ritual.

Some nights, Reginald would lie awake, wondering if tomorrow he might wake up with money under his pillow, maybe left by a tooth fairy who had navigated the desert just for him. He believed it when his grandmother said that there was magic only if you had faith. Magic that explained everything the world didn't: why babies arrived suddenly in the night (dropped by airplanes while the family slept), why whirlwinds twisted across their yards (spirits demanding knives pointed skyward), and why those city kids always returned fresh, neat, and full of stories he could barely imagine.

Every morning, the first bus would rumble from the edges of the village just as the sun cracked over the dunes, carrying away those lucky enough to learn things of far and beyond.

Reginald's school feet were calloused. His uniform was a hand-me-down. His currency was resilience, even when his stomach rumbled. Even when he couldn't afford the school trip. Even when classmates called him "nothing" for having nothing, he walked on.

Moving Up

At school, nobody asked how he felt. Even at home, his mother barely paid him any attention. Not until his aunt came home, the one from the boarding school. She was a flicker of city light in his rural dusk. She asked about his day. She gave him sweets if he showed her what he'd written. She touched his world like rain touches drought—momentary, but life-altering. And when she left again, her absence was loud. But the memory of her curiosity and her faith in him stayed.

He carried that faith like a secret. It whispered that he was not just a barefoot boy, not just a child without coins. He was something else. He was more.

At home, there was always work. He chopped wood before he read books. Carried water before he carried dreams. And still, when his grandmother spoke beside the fire, telling tales of cunning animals and distant lands, he listened with wonder. Her voice sounded like protection, like she could wrap her words around him and shield him from the world's crueler truths.

His father, when present, was a quiet man of strict lines and few words. Reginald once jumped the locked gate to find him, only to be met not with a hug, but a lesson: "Next time, wait. Scream my name. Don't jump." So Reginald learned. Learned when to speak. When to stay silent. How to knock at the door without making a sound.

Yet, he never begged. Never asked for more than was offered. It was pride, yes, but also something deeper—a code passed down from his grandmother. "Don't ask," her hands seemed to say when they tucked in his shirt or placed food before him. "Become."

He began to see the world differently. City lights weren't promises anymore. They had also become lies. Yet, they called to him. But back in Pella, they were described as danger. Cities were the places where boys disappeared, where dreams got eaten whole. So, he dreamed carefully. Softly. Like someone who didn't want the dream to break.

He didn't know where he was going. He only knew he couldn't stay still.

At night, he'd stare across the dark expanse of the sky, flickering with artificial stars. A child in the bush, seeing the glint of something he couldn't name—not yet. But he would. One day. Somehow.

Joy wasn't in what he had. It was in how he lived. Without shoes. Without maps. But never without wonder.

And now, decades later, he carried that wonder like an ember inside him. A man in polished shoes, walking hotel corridors, helping guests sip fine wines and speak of other continents. But when he touched the doorknob to his office or greeted a stranger in a starched white shirt, a part of him was still running—barefoot, free, dust-kissed— through the hot sand and wild grass of Pella.

That boy had not died.

He had merely grown taller, stronger, wiser.

The boy who once chased chickens from the path of a whirlwind had never seen the city, yet somehow, he already missed it.

It started with the distant lights. Pinpricks on the horizon, trembling against the black canvas of the Kalahari night. Reginald didn't know their source—only that they meant something. The adults called it "Upington" or sometimes just "town," as if it were another planet where shoes were worn, people bathed in bathtubs, and bread came in plastic, not from ashes and iron pots. In the village, lights were stories. Each glimmer was a rumor, a prayer, a map etched in stars and longing. What the city actually was didn't matter—it mattered only that it wasn't *here*.

He didn't know what he was missing, only that he was missing something.

The first time he asked about the lights, his uncle laughed. "That's where people go to disappear," he said. That stuck. The way superstitions do. The way wounds do. The city became a myth, a monster, and a miracle, all wrapped in one. A place feared by the old and dreamt of by the young.

But Reginald didn't want to disappear. He wanted to appear—fully, completely, in a world where he didn't have to look down at his feet to remember where he came from. A world where his voice didn't feel borrowed. A world where he carried his own identity and individuality.

The first time he heard a city bus roar past the edge of the village, it shook the ground beneath him. Reginald was only five. It was just an engine—old, grinding, diesel-stinking—but to him it sounded like freedom, like something unstoppable. He would watch the bus vanish in a dust trail, carrying strangers toward a world he could only imagine. And then, he'd walk back home barefoot, legs coated in ochre soil, thinking of the lives beyond the horizon—ones that wore socks, carried briefcases, and didn't wake to roosters.

He didn't know the word for "aspiration" then. But he felt it.

The city, for all its danger, was still a possibility to Reginald. His dreams weren't cinematic or oversized. They were humble. Shoes that didn't blister. A haircut that didn't draw blood. A mirror that didn't mock him with the hollowness of lack. He was never greedy for luxury. All he ever craved was dignity.

"I just want to go there," he once told his grandmother.

She had looked at him, eyes filled with old sorrow. "My boy," she said, "the city is not built for soft hearts."

And yet, she softened her heart just enough to let him keep dreaming. She didn't feed his fantasy, but she never crushed it either. That was her gift—to allow the seed of belief to take root, even if the soil was dry.

That belief lit him from within. In school, while others stared out the window with resignation, he stared with curiosity. His handwriting was uneven, his shoes non-existent, but his attention? Sharpened by hunger—for *more*. He didn't know what he'd become, only that he *would* become.

His aunt asked questions no one had ever asked. "How was school? What did you learn?" He froze, shy. No one had ever inquired like that. It was foreign, like trying to speak in a language you didn't know you were allowed to use.

But he answered. Clumsily, softly, like a bird learning its first song.

Those brief chapters of her visits, her sweets, and her belief lit something irreversible inside him. When she vanished back to the city, he felt it in his chest like an open window left in the wind. But she had left him with a vision, not just of the city, but of *himself*—better, bolder, belonging somewhere beyond the red dust of Pella.

The lights returned every evening. Distant. Flickering. But no longer abstract.

They were calling.

And one day, he would answer.

Years later, standing in a hotel lobby wrapped in five-star air-conditioning and the constant lull of violins through hidden speakers, Reginald would remember how it felt to watch the lights from afar. He would think about the way elders had warned him—"It'll eat you alive"—and realize they had been both wrong and right.

The city had swallowed him. But not to destroy him. To reveal him.

Every hallway he walked in, wearing dress shoes, every room he opened with a master key, was a manifestation of a barefoot boy who once believed that airplanes dropped babies, and who made wishes at the sky, not knowing anyone could hear.

He still didn't have a map. But he had made one from memory. From scars. From longing.

And the lights? They no longer lived in the distance.

They lived around him.

There were mornings when Reginald walked into his office and didn't recognize the air. It had shifted somehow—grown colder, quieter, like it was waiting for him to leave. No one said it outright, of course. That's not how exclusion often works. It's in the pauses, the invisible recalibrations of space. It's in the way people stop laughing when you enter, in the smile that seems forced.

At Cheetah Plains, the architecture was impeccable, featuring glass, timber, and stone. But Reginald knew beauty could be deceiving. Even a place that looks like it belongs in a magazine can push you to the margins. One day, his office was moved without any explanation. "Your desk is now... anywhere," someone had said with a shrug. It landed like a slap cloaked in silk.

He didn't say anything then. Didn't ask why. He had learned not to. Asking meant exposing a wound that others insisted wasn't there.

But he felt it. Oh, he felt it.

There is a loneliness that lives beneath polished surfaces—one that gnaws quietly, like rust in steel. Reginald had walked a long way from Pella, yet some days it felt like he was still standing outside, waiting to be invited in. He had learned the language, mastered the posture, and even become an expert, and still, he was sometimes seen as a guest in a room he had helped build.

How strange, he thought, to be celebrated and sidelined in the same breath.

Back in Pella, at least you knew where you stood. Poverty had no illusions. You were barefoot and you were poor, but you were not questioned. You were not misread. You were not asked to smile through erasure.

In the lodge, people marveled at the wines he selected, the way he described tannins and terroir like a man reciting poetry. They admired his memory, his palate. But admiration is not the same as acceptance. They clapped for his knowledge. But they didn't always sit next to him when the workday ended. They toasted his recommendations, but not his presence.

And yet, he stayed. He worked. He rose.

Only because he had promised himself—and that barefoot boy—that he would not quit. That he would not let anyone's discomfort with his presence subtract him from his own life.

He carried his grandmother's voice like a spine beneath his suit. *My child, one day you'll grow to be a man. A good man.* Her words kept him rooted. Deep enough to hold him upright in rooms that tried to make him small.

He had grown used to being both seen and unseen. He could dazzle at a wine tasting and still feel like furniture. He could shake hands with billionaires and still ache to be asked how his day was, not because of a customer survey, but because someone actually cared.

Belonging, he realized, is not about where you are. It is about recognition. And for people like him, recognition is often rationed, offered in teaspoons and taken back in buckets.

Still, he never let it harden him. He couldn't afford to. Bitterness is a heavy thing to carry, and he had already walked too far.

So he smiled. He gave more than he took. And every time someone tried to make him small, he stood a little taller, not to intimidate, but to remind himself that he had earned every inch of ground he stood on.

And though he sometimes felt like he was squatting in someone else's dream, he knew this truth in his bones:

He had built his place, not borrowed it.

And maybe, just maybe, belonging wasn't a destination. Perhaps it was a wound, one that never quite closed, but taught you how to walk anyway.

With grace. With memory. With defiance wrapped in kindness.

He never wanted to forget. Not the dust, not the barefoot mornings, not the boy who spoke more to the wind than to people. Reginald learned early that forgetting isn't healing—it's erasure. And he had come too far, fought too quietly, endured too deeply to erase anything. He remembered it all as proof. Proof that he had lived, and that he had mattered, even when the world barely noticed.

In hotel lobbies, his name was pronounced crisply. His title preceded him like a ribbon of importance. There were nods of approval. Glasses raised. Guests who marveled at his knowledge, his precision, and his calm. But none of that ever made him feel bigger than the boy who once ran under skies so wide they seemed to swallow sorrow whole. That boy still stood beside him as a guide.

He often thought of the mirror—not the one in the suite bathroom or the gleaming silver one behind the bar, but the one that lived in silence. The inner mirror – his conscience. The one that didn't care for polished shoes or name tags. That mirror didn't flatter. It remembered. It remembered the child who smelled rain before it fell. Who knew the difference between the whistle of a dove and the cry of hunger? Who made peace with hunger because there was no choice, and who never let that peace become complacency.

Even now, when he ties his tie or answers to "Sir," there's a flicker. Not self-doubt—no, that's too small. It's something larger, something ancient. A tether to origins, to grit, to the sacred ordinariness of survival. He doesn't flinch when he feels it. He honors it. Because he knows: success didn't rescue him. He rescued himself.

There are still days when he feels like a misfit in a tailored life. Still moments when a stare lingers too long, when a laugh skips past him, when a decision is made as if he's not in the room. Belonging, he's learned, is not granted. It is carved—sometimes painfully—into the walls of spaces never built for people like him. And yet, he remains. Not as an intruder. But as an anchor.

He walks gently. Not because he fears breaking anything, but because he understands what it feels like to be broken. He doesn't demand space. He earns it—word by word, act by act, silence by silence. And in doing so, he keeps that barefoot boy alive. That boy who once stood beneath airplanes and whispered, "Take me with you."

Reginald never left him behind.

The boy is in the way; he refuses to eat alone if someone else is hungry. In the way he greets the cleaner before the CEO. In the way he stands a little too long in doorways, remembering all the doors that were once shut. That boy is not a memory—he is marrow. And every time Reginald chooses kindness over pride, patience over proof, humility over applause, he's not just surviving. He's declaring, 'I am still here.'

In a world that measures worth in decimals and diplomas, he wears his past as scripture and his childhood as education. It taught him to hear beyond words, to read the room before reading the menu, to know who needed comfort by the way they held their coffee cup.

Sometimes, late at night, when the guests have gone quiet and the stars return to their posts, he sits alone and smiles. Not because everything is perfect, but because he knows who he is. Not despite his past. Because of it.

Chapter 2: Desert Beginnings in Pella

The rain pelted quietly and soaked the red soil of his homeland. Reginald woke up before the sun, before the roosters. Barefoot, he slipped out of his bed and went outside to see the rain, to measure the intensity and the weight of the water droplets, and to calculate the amount of struggle he would have to do today in order to survive.

The little boy rushed inside and grabbed an empty bucket from the washroom area. His bare feet ran as fast as they could to save as many drops of water as he could from getting wasted on the soil. He needed to conserve the rainwater so he wouldn't have to travel a mile to fetch a bucket.

With his cold hands and calloused feet, he brought the bucket and placed it in the open courtyard. The animals were sleeping, yet he could hear humans in the neighborhood waking up to save the water, to save the day.

The man in the suit, sitting at his table, sipping his coffee, could still hear the morning sound of pouring rain and running feet. He was in the lodge, yet he was living in those days of his childhood when he would wake up before the birds and get ready for the day. The wristwatch on his hand looked up at him with timid glances. It admired the little boy who beat the time.

After placing the bucket, he ran inside and began to prepare wood for the fire so his grandmother could cook something for the family to eat. Not for breakfast, though. In his homeland, where hunger was the government, people did not have breakfast or lunch. They only had dinners blended with love and some spices that his grandmother would feed everyone while telling dinner-time stories. The man in the suit still did not do breakfasts or lunches. He still only ate at night. And that was the "normal" for him.

"I need to leave for school early or else I wouldn't make it," young Reginald said to himself as he grabbed his worn-out uniform from the clothing line. The drizzle had lightly soaked the uniform, he realized. The man in the suit smiled, shaking his head as the young Reginald shook the uniform to dry it as much as he could.

The drizzle faded slowly, giving way to a pale, slow sunrise. The boy, still brushing droplets off his damp uniform, glanced toward the fence where the donkeys were tied. They stood quietly, their ears twitching, swatting away the early flies. They would soon have their duty.

He stepped barefoot over the smooth patches of dry mud near the shed and shouted softly, "Mpho! Mpho, wake up!"

From the side of the hut, a small voice responded with a grunt. Then came the sound of shuffling feet and a yawn that belonged to someone used to being woken up before the sky turned blue.

"Reginald... It's Saturday," Mpho mumbled, rubbing his eyes.

"I know," Reginald replied. "But Mama said we must fetch wood early. The pump isn't working again. We'll go with the donkeys. You bring the ropes."

There was no time to delay. The donkeys had to be harnessed before the sun began its climb, before the air turned from cold to cruel. By the time Mpho came out dragging the ropes, the young boy had already pulled the small wooden cart into the open, its one wheel squeaking with memory.

"You think they'll give us firewood again near the old mission?" Mpho asked as he tightened the knot around the donkey's front leg.

Reginald nodded. "They always do when it's cold. They said we can use the fallen ones."

They moved quickly, attaching the cart and adjusting the harness made of old fabric and leather straps. It was not elegant, but it worked. The donkeys understood the pulse of need.

In the silence between echoes, the man in the suit turned his head back toward the courtyard, where the tin bucket caught each falling drop with a soft metallic echo.

Moving Up

Sitting beside a window, the suit too sharp for comfort, the coffee turned cold as memories pulled him back.

He heard a voice—his own, younger voice—saying:

"Mama, why must we go so far for water? Why can't the pump just stay alive?"

And Mama, always calm, would answer with a shrug,

"Because the people who fix the pumps don't live in Pella, my child."

Back in the boy's world, the cart was ready. They were moving. Mpho hopped on the back, and Reginald guided the donkeys through the narrow, winding path that cut through the village. He spoke to them just as he would to friends.

"Tsamaea, Lefa. Tsamaea…"

The hooves of the donkeys drummed on the hardened ground, each thud in time with the boy's thoughts. He had no shoes. The soles of his feet were leathered by the earth. He was not afraid of the journey. Not afraid of the thorns or the cracked land. But school... that was something else.

He dreaded school for the language that his teachers forced him to speak. Words with sharp edges—English, Afrikaans—each day they tried to force those into his tongue like fitting rocks into a river's mouth.

"Jou naam (your name)*?" the teacher would ask.*

Reginald would hesitate. "Uh… Reginald."

The class would laugh. He would look down in embarrassment and pretend not to hear.

Inside his home, his voice was strong. His mother tongue danced like fire around their evening meals. But inside that classroom, his voice became a whisper, dry as the winter grass.

Even Mpho knew.

"You said *ke lapile* today when the teacher asked you in Afrikaans," Mpho teased once. "She looked confused."

"I don't care," Reginald had muttered, looking away. "Let her learn too."

That unspoken resistance would harden over time. But for now, there was still wood to gather. Still water to chase. Still feet to toughen.

And somewhere far ahead—across years, through uniforms, across languages and broken pumps—there was a man in a suit who still hadn't learned to forget these things.

Not the cart.

Not the donkeys.

Not the cold drizzle in Pella.

Not the barefoot boy who beat the time.

The donkeys were tied up under the marula tree by midday. Reginald wiped his forehead with the back of his hand, then rubbed his fingers together and noticed the fine film of ash from the firewood. He didn't mind. It meant something had been done. Something useful.

By the time he reached the house, the sun had taken its rightful place on the throne of the sky. Grandmother had already begun boiling water in the soot-blackened kettle. The uniform was dry now, sun-scorched and slightly stiff. He slipped into it without ceremony. A boy didn't need comfort; he needed purpose.

School was waiting. He was already late.

The long walk began. Feet slapping the ground, eyes fixed on the road, but thoughts always trailing elsewhere. It was not just a walk. It was a ritual, during which he used to dream about tiled floors, big cars, bustling cities, and English-speaking men in suits.

The older Reginald, dressed in a suit, smiled sadly as he reminisced about his younger self.

Inside the small schoolhouse, heat absorbed into the corrugated walls like an uninvited ghost. Desks creaked. Chalk dust floated in the stale air. And there it was—*the book*. He never despised anything more.

Thick. Heavy. With a brown and green cover that had seen better decades.

General Science.

It was the only book that every child of that time from Pella could recognize blindfolded. A textbook that asked a boy to understand the muscles of a frog and the formula for gravity, while the village itself offered no running water and no electricity.

The teacher, an old man with a voice like broken branches, would say:

"Open to page thirty-two. The hydrological cycle."

But Reginald's eyes would wander. Outside, across the dry field, he could see the donkeys from earlier grazing quietly. That, too, was science. That, too, was a cycle.

Biblical Studies came next. And there was no escaping it. Psalms and parables. Jonah and the whale. Names that lived in stories more vivid than the people around him. It wasn't the belief he wrestled with, it was how it was taught. How all things, even God, came in lessons.

Afrikaans followed. That language, thick and dry on the tongue like uncooked maize meal, always stung him. Mistakes meant shame mispronunciations meant laughter. But still, he listened. Still, he repeated and reminded himself that he spoke Afrikaans better than English.

His mother tongue was never a subject of study. It was a whisper between friends. A code shared in the courtyard while dodging prefects and avoiding the long arm of punishment. It was what they spoke when they dreamed. And dreams, back then, were small and communal.

"You, me, Abby, even Mpho, we're gonna finish school and build our own place. Just there by the hills," said one of his classmates once, eyes squinting toward a patch of land far beyond the footpath.

Reginald had nodded. Not because he believed it, but because belief was all they had.

But even then, something in him had begun to twitch. He heard the other languages—the thunder of Zulu, the river-tone of Xhosa—and he listened not with fear but with hunger. He mimicked the tones in secret. Practiced them when no one was watching. Collected syllables the way other boys collected bottle caps.

And the English? That old stone in his shoe? He polished it. Bit by bit. Word by word. Like shining a rusty coin in hopes that it might one day buy freedom.

Still, the dreams... those bright, unruly dreams, they came in flashes, like lightning over dry land. And just as quickly, they disappeared.

What dream could you hold onto in a place where roofs leaked and pumps broke and the biggest book in the classroom held all the subjects of the world—but none of its tenderness?

Reginald walked home that evening with a silent heart. He watched the sky change. The clouds gather again. The smell of dust and rain returning.

He did not yet dream of cities or suits. But something in him, some small, defiant ember, had seen the world once, in the way you see a chameleon in a basket of Smarties. Not to understand it. Not to catch it. Just to know that something colorful and strange existed.

And that maybe, one day, he would touch it.

The older man in a suit took his cup of coffee, all cold and stale, and went to the bookshelf. He would still drink that cup. His grandmother, the lovely woman who taught him ways of life, never taught him to waste a bit of food. Where he came from, food was never taken forsaken as it was only served once a day.

He could sit and think about thousands of such days, yet he would never cry about it. They had made him who he was today.

Moving Up

At this age, he usually preferred to stay alone in quietude. However, he liked to remember and romanticize about his childhood friends and how they played a crucial role in building him.

Reginald was maybe 12 or 13 when he finally moved to the city where his mother already lived. Leaving his childhood friends and his loving grandmother was not an easy pill to swallow, yet he had dreams that called him to the other side.

The train that took him to the city wasn't a train at all. It was a rusty pickup, coughing black smoke, with bags tied in ropes and goats crying in the back. Reginald sat near the edge of the open bed, gripping the side, staring ahead as the dirt roads melted into something firmer, something called *tar*.

The city didn't announce itself with words. It crept in with lights and noise, with the smell of burning petrol and roasted meat, with buildings that had no corners of silence. He had not arrived *in* the city. He had arrived *close enough* to it. On its outer skin. A place that pulsed with everything new and untranslatable.

His mother met him just past the taxi rank. Her voice was the same. Her hug was smaller, or maybe he had grown. She handed him a new uniform. Gray trousers, light blue shirt, a badge he didn't recognize stitched into the pocket.

"This is your school now," she said. "You'll like it here. They have a big library too."

That night, he lay on a thin mattress in a rented backroom with cracked windows. Through the gaps in the curtain, the city blinked at him, streetlamps and passing headlights like messages in Morse code. He had never seen so many lights glowing in the night sky at the same time before. It looked like daytime. Back in the village, the nights would be dark, and if they had lights like this, they would spend the nights harvesting too.

Older Reginald sighed and switched off the extra lights in the room. He only kept the ones open that he needed to read a book.

Teenage Reginald didn't sleep much that night. Not because he wasn't tired. But because everything buzzed. The air itself seemed awake, as though the city had swallowed a drum and couldn't stop beating.

School was the first jolt.

The kids walked with a different move. Their shoes were clean. They spoke fast English, sometimes Afrikaans, sometimes something else he couldn't catch. Their jokes didn't land the same way. Their eyes didn't always meet his. But their hands moved like his. Their hunger was different, not for food, but for something unnamed. They had the kind of freedom that village children couldn't even dream of because they didn't know the word for it.

Then came my friend with the wild hair and the laugh that broke all silence. Who walked him past school gates and into hidden arcades behind convenience stores, where machines blinked and beeped like they were alive. The first time Reginald touched the plastic buttons, he felt the same electricity that had buzzed in the city's air. He had lost the first game in seconds. His friend laughed. He smiled. A smile that reached back to the barefoot boy measuring rain in a bucket.

"What do you think?" he had asked.

Reginald squinted at the screen. "It's like magic. But real."

And that's how the city taught him. Not with books, but with color. Not with lessons, but with moments. In the village, he had memorized the hydrological cycle. Here, he learned the cycle of buses. The cycle of theft. The cycle of chasing something, anything, even if you didn't know what it was.

In those fast-paced moments of city life, Reginald missed his village friend Abby. After school, they would race bottle caps on sidewalks. Make imaginary maps of imaginary worlds. They climbed trees where birds had learned to sing above the noise. They drew chalk lines on mud pavements that no one cared to wash away. His grandmother used to laugh and say that these kind of games makes one's mind sharper.

However, looking back, it feels like he lived in a desert. Horrible and peaceful at the same time. But the man in polished shoes was grateful to have lived that part of life—it shaped who he was today.

The city was different. It made him feel stimulated and alive. For the first time, Reginald's mind was not fenced in.

He started dreaming again, not about donkeys or rain buckets or building an empire in the village, but about strange new things. Dreams with buttons and pixels. Dreams with questions. Why did some kids live in tall buildings while others shared one mattress? Why did some speak as if the world was theirs, and others spoke as if they were borrowing it?

And yet, he wasn't bitter.

He still remembered where he came from. That desert of peace and hardship. That dust-colored silence that had shaped the bones inside him.

Now, the noise sharpened his edges.

He walked slower than the other boys, but he listened deeper. He didn't shout like them, but he remembered everything. He still didn't eat breakfast or lunch. But now he *understood* why. Hunger was not just in the belly. It was in the bones. It was in the silence that followed every question left unanswered.

The city had not made him soft. It had made him aware.

And under the fluorescent flicker of arcade lights, beside the only friend who truly saw him as something more than a quiet boy in a secondhand uniform, Reginald felt a shift, an invisible tether pulling him toward something bigger.

He didn't know its name yet. But it felt like the world had opened its door a crack.

And Reginald was standing at the threshold, listening.

It started quietly, like most things that grow teeth in the shadows. With everything good comes the bad hand in hand.

One afternoon, he and one of his schoolmates had taken a longer walk after school, past the arcades, past the bus station, into a part of the city where the houses leaned like they were tired and the air smelled of heat and rust. That's where he met the other boys—older, louder, with eyes that didn't blink often.

They didn't wear school uniforms. Their days weren't divided into lessons and bells. They knew other rhythms: the rhythm of police sirens, of dodging responsibilities, of lighting a match with your thumbnail.

Reginald stood among them once, maybe twice. Curious, unsure. There was something magnetic about them, not because of what they had, but because of how little they seemed to need. They laughed with empty stomachs and full lungs, passed bottles without looking, lit rolled paper with fingers that didn't tremble.

He was 13 when someone handed him a cigarette.

His friend had raised an eyebrow. "Sure, you want to try that?"

He shrugged. He wasn't trying to impress. He was trying to understand.

The smoke hit his throat like ashwater. His lungs folded. His body bent forward in a cough that felt like betrayal.

They laughed. He laughed too, half ashamed, half relieved that it didn't suit him.

Then came the green paper, the rolled joint with the pungent truth curled inside. He remembered the texture more than the taste, how the world tilted, not in a poetic way, but like a spinning bucket on the edge of a table. Dizzy, senseless, hollow.

That night, he came home quiet.

His mother was waiting. She didn't need a confession. Mothers know the language of the body, the stutter of a guilty footstep, the silence that hangs too low in the throat.

The spanking wasn't cruel. It was clear. A sentence written in open palm.

"That is not who you are," she said. No yelling. Just that, her calm and steady tone, telling him she knew him more than he could ever know himself.

And somehow, that cut deeper. Slowly, she came towards him and bent down. His dilated, ashamed eyes watched as his mother quietly picked up a big stick from the ground and held it tight in her hand. He closed his eyes and braced himself as his mother spanked him. Not a shiver or shriek of pain escaped his throat, and he went to bed with his head bent low in shame.

That was the only time.

He never touched it again, not because of the pain, but because he saw what it could do. Not just to the lungs, eyes, or grades. But to *dreams*. How it gnawed at the edges of possibility. How it turned the sharp boys into shadows.

Some of those boys didn't make it past 17.

Others walked with a slowness that had nothing to do with pace and everything to do with what they were carrying inside them.

Reginald never judged.

He didn't laugh at the boys who lit their mornings with smoke or poured their evenings into brown bottles. He understood. Life in the city was beautiful in a cracked, violent way. It offered you neon lights, but no map. It sang to you in broken radios, but never gave you a lullaby.

Some boys were just looking for quiet.

But Reginald wanted more.

He still walked slowly. Still wore his uniform like armor. Still came home to a small room with peeling walls and a mother who watched everything in silence. But inside him, the bucket from the village still stood, collecting not rainwater now, but moments. Lessons. Warnings. Questions.

He still hadn't learned how to dream out loud. But he had learned to *protect* the dream that flickered inside him like a candle cupped in two hands.

The street was no longer just a road.

It had become a choice.

And every step young Reginald took to become the man he was now was deliberate.

The dust had barely settled on the shoes Reginald wore when he first arrived in the city, yet already the world around him had begun to shift again.

It was the mid-90s. South Africa stood at the mouth of something new and uncertain. The country had changed its name, its anthem, and its face. But for the boys who walked through its classrooms in secondhand shoes and with heavy silences, change came slower. More quietly. Like a new language trying to learn how to speak itself.

In those days, especially in the Northwest and northern parts of South Africa, the African languages were taught only as a second language, if at all. Apartheid still lingered in the air, like smoke that refused to lift. Afrikaans came with authority, English with obligation. And buried underneath was the vernacular, their mother tongue, spoken softly between friends, passed like notes under a desk, never written on the chalkboard.

The man in the suit could still feel the pain crawling up his spine as his thoughts went deep into the apartheid times.

Young Reginald grew up with friends bound not by blood, but by belief and trust. Boys like Eric, Tumelo, and Isaac. Together, they were shaped by red dust, cold mornings, and dreams they didn't yet have words for. They carried each other, not just in friendship, but in faith, that they would all make it. That the rubble around them could still be built into something permanent. A future. An empire. Back home. Something of their own.

Then came 1994. The apartheid had ended.

The year the map changed, and so did they. The collapse of Bophuthatswana tore holes in their routines, and with it, their sense of direction. Suddenly, school became a place of fire instead of pencils. Tires burned. Classrooms emptied. Uniforms folded in drawers like relics of a lost era.

Moving Up

The man in the suit put his book down and shut his eyes, as if keeping them open would burn them with hot tears boiling inside.

The school children waited. Waited for the noise to die down. Waited for someone to say it was okay to be a child again. But childhood does not pause; it shifts. And theirs shifted into something heavier. Fear became common. Some parents kept their children home for good, believing danger had too many ways of entering a school gate. Others, like Reginald's mother, sent them anyway—because what choice was there?

When school finally reopened after Nelson Mandela's election, the buildings were the same, but the people were not. Desks sat empty where laughter once lived. Some of Reginald's friends never came back. Not because they had died, but because something inside them had. The fire had singed their will, and they grew into other shapes, followed other paths. Some began working early. Others drifted into silence.

Eric stopped wearing his uniform. His shoes became covered in layers of construction dust. Isaac began helping his uncle sell fruit on the roadside. Tumelo simply vanished and moved away to stay with a cousin in another part of the country.

Reginald kept walking to school. Slower now. Always counting who was missing. Always sitting beside the same window, hoping maybe, just maybe, they'd come back.

Yet even when they lost the classroom, they never lost the play.

In the streets, they became warriors, inventors, and kings with cardboard crowns. They played games older than fences. Games with names passed down like family secrets, played with flat stones, torn footballs, twisted wires, and tin cans turned into treasure. They didn't have instructions. They had instinct.

When apartheid ruined almost everything, it could not ruin their trust in friendship. Even the boys who dropped out joined in after school hours. Their language was laughter. Their rules were unwritten. That's how culture survived: quietly, through repetition, through joy. They didn't need to understand the origin of a game to know how to carry it forward.

But inside the new South Africa, a new order had arrived.

Classrooms buzzed with the unfamiliar hum of mixed tongues. Xhosa and Zulu walked the same corridors as Afrikaans and English. A Black child could now sit beside a white one, though neither truly knew what to say.

The teachers changed, too. Some brought new methods. Some clung tightly to old punishments. Reginald remembered a teacher once who paused in the middle of a lesson and asked if they were ready to live in a country that wouldn't wait for them. Reginald didn't answer. He just traced the edge of his desk with his finger. He was fourteen, still learning what it meant to raise a hand for the right reasons.

Around that time, he began to read in a different way. Not just the words in class, but the city itself. He watched how people stood in queues, how some pushed forward, how others stepped back. He listened to conversations at bus stops. Noticed how grown men lowered their voices when they spoke of jobs.

School was no longer just about finishing. Life was now about reading the world correctly.

Still, there were moments that softened the noise.

Saturday soccer games were played in dusty fields with stacked bricks as goalposts. Laughter that echoed past barbed-wire fences. The taste of vetkoek fried in reused oil. The rare, golden luxury of a cold drink from a spaza shop fridge, even if it had to be split three ways. They would still dive and swim in the muddy water, splashing each other under the scorching sun.

And the nights—yes, the cold nights—when the world shrank to a single candle, a single radio voice speaking softly about what tomorrow might bring. His mother would iron his uniform beneath a flickering bulb. He'd sit on the floor, doing homework with three languages fighting for space in his head—Afrikaans, English, and Setswana. Some nights, he didn't know which one his dreams would choose. Maybe all of them. Maybe none.

But the dreams never left him.

Moving Up

He still carried his grandmother's voice in his ears. Still heard Mpho calling from the yard. Still remembered the sound of donkeys walking through dawn. Even in the city's humming heartbeat, those memories were louder.

The older man in the suit put the book back on the shelf and buttoned up his suit. His eyes were still wet from the grim memories of apartheid. The thought of his grandmother would arouse a bittersweet feeling inside his chest. She was someone who taught him the ways of life, and these books could never.

He sat back down in his office chair and reclined a little. His eyelids closed automatically, and his mind jumped on another wagon down the memory lane.

Back then, no one in Reginald's world could afford a real soccer ball. But poverty had never stopped play; it simply reshaped it. The boys would collect plastic bags scattered around the village, gather them with threads and twine, wrap them tighter and tighter until they formed something round. It wasn't a ball. But it was enough. They kicked it across dusty fields until the layers unraveled, the insides torn like overplayed laughter. That was the signal—the game was over.

There were other games, too. The timeless ones. Hide and seek behind tin shacks or termite mounds. Spinning a coin, calling heads or tails. That last one, the grown-ups called gambling. Forbidden. But boys are made of curiosity, and sometimes mischief. They played anyway, in corners where adult eyes couldn't reach. Reginald and his closest friends would giggle and whisper their bets, even though they rarely had anything to bet with. Still, they played—not for money, but for pride, for bragging rights, for the thrill of being just a little bit naughty.

There were days when they skipped school together.

It was never a solo act. Always a collective agreement, like an unwritten rule passed around at sunrise.

"Today, we disappear."

And disappear they did. Into the bush, slipping away while other children marched in lines to schoolyards. Summer made everything possible. The wild pool beyond the thorn trees called to them. Nobody owned a swimming pool back then. What they had were small river bends or rain-fed ponds, muddy but magical. They would leap in, splash like kings, and laugh until their voices broke into coughs.

They came back home soaked in laughter. Or worse, dry, sun-baked, and ghost-like. Sometimes barefoot. Sometimes, wearing the wrong clothes. They'd run when caught, grabbing whatever shirt or shorts they could find—clothes left behind in panic. Sometimes Reginald would come home wearing Tumelo's shirt, and Isaac would be in someone else's too-small trousers. No one asked questions. Everyone knew.

Those were the wild days. The ones too loud to forget.

But it wasn't all mischief. There were traditions, too—things passed down like sacred recipes, stirred slowly in iron pots and remembered in the belly long after the day had ended.

Reginald's grandmother cooked with wisdom. Her hands knew the story of the soil. One of her most beloved dishes was made from corn and beans, two humble ingredients, dried and stored for winter, then simmered for hours until they softened. The maize had to be harvested early, while still green, or roasted over an open flame when fresh. When dried, it was ground or boiled. The beans, too, were sun-cured until they rattled like stones in a basket. Then, together, they became a dish that could silence hunger with half a bowl.

Food, in their home, was medicine. It filled not only the stomach, but the spirit. Reginald swore that a plate of those corn-and-bean meals could chase away every ache of the day. And it did.

In other seasons, the bush became the market. They'd head out, barefoot, hunting not animals, but fruit. Bucha fruits grew wild, hanging low enough to pluck but high enough to compete with the monkeys. Sometimes, they fought those monkeys for a prize berry. Sometimes, they lost. It didn't matter. There were always wild berries, fat with flavor, growing where the dust couldn't reach.

There were more than five kinds—maybe more than ten—but Reginald only ever knew their names in his own language. They had a taste only the village tongue could describe. Names, like poetry, passed through generations, but never written down. Nature gave them freely, and the boys took without guilt. No one talked of vitamins or nutrition. They just ate. And they stayed strong.

Then came the Mopani worms.

Only during the Christmas season. Only when the butterflies laid their eggs and vanished, leaving behind the strange, fat larvae that would become a delicacy, the little Reginald loved them. The worms came in November, crawling like secrets across the leaves. They were gathered, cleaned, cooked, and sometimes dried. People in northern South Africa, in parts of Zimbabwe and Mozambique, all knew their worth.

They weren't seen as strange or disgusting. They were tradition. Protein was packed in memory. Reginald still ate them, even as a grown man. Still savored them like delicacies in the finest restaurant. Because they *were*. Not just food. They were strength. Health. Immunity before anyone ever said the word "vitamin." They were medicine without a prescription.

He had never known steak back then. Never tasted it. But he never felt lacking. Because what they ate came from the earth, from the trees, from the fire his grandmother lit every night.

Even now, as a man, he would choose those dishes. Corn and beans. Roasted maize. Wild berries. Mopani worms.

Because they were more than food. They were the taste of home.

And the taste of survival. The man in the suit, sitting comfortably in his reclined office chair, knew very well that he had survived well enough to be able to live this life.

Chapter 3: Barefoot Schooldays

It was almost time to go back to his home, where his family awaited him. He stood up from the office chair and picked up his briefcase from the office table. The buttoned suit was suffocating him, and the child who still lived inside him. As soon as he got to his car, he took off his tuxedo and threw it in the back seat along with the briefcase.

The sun was almost down when he arrived home. There was still time for dinner, so he decided to wait in his study. His grandmother had taught him to be patient regarding food and instilled in him a kind of calm that still kept him grounded.

Whenever he thought about the good times in the village, his mind automatically went back to the grim city life, the city that took his soul.

Life in the city, for Reginald, did not begin with wonder or wide-eyed excitement. There were no tall buildings that made him pause or lights so dazzling they erased the past. It was, in many ways, simply a change in address. The same rhythm of waking early, the same long walks to school, the same weight of responsibility on young shoulders. Only now, the dust had been replaced by tar, and the silence of the bush by the constant hum of engines and conversation.

He was thirteen when he moved in with his mother and stepfather. The room they shared was small but functional, with electricity that flickered during storms but still felt like a luxury after village nights spent under the rule of dim candlelight. It was not perfect, but it was something new. For young Reginald, the dim light was enough to see dreams

His stepfather was a quiet man with a tired face, the kind that had memorized the inside of mine shafts more intimately than the inside of his own home. He worked hard, and drank harder. After long shifts underground, he'd come home, take off his boots with a sigh, and pour himself a drink. On weekends, the drinking stretched longer, his voice louder, his footsteps heavier. But he was not cruel. Reginald would say even now, after all these years, that the man had a good heart, just one that had been worn down by hard work and low wages.

They were not poor in spirit, but the pockets told a different story. Money came and went too quickly, and though the family never went to bed starving, luxuries were few. Someone, somewhere, helped them make ends meet. Reginald never knew the details, but it was still a tightrope walk. Each month, a balancing act of what could be paid and what had to wait.

His mother, though loving, had expectations that never softened. As the eldest, Reginald became the second parent by default. His younger brother was already living with them, and not long after Reginald's arrival, a new voice joined the household—a baby sister, born of his mother and stepfather. She came into the world without asking, but her presence redrew the lines of duty. Reginald's list of chores grew longer.

Every Saturday, his mother would hand him a worn paper list, neatly written in her careful script. Off he would go, walking to town through busy streets and narrow alleys, passing vendors and stray dogs and other boys with looser schedules. He never complained. It was life, and he had learned not to expect it to be fair.

But there was one small rebellion—so minor it almost didn't count. Every now and then, he would buy himself a can of spray deodorant with the change from his groceries. It wasn't fancy, just a small can of scent, the kind other boys seemed to wear without effort. Reginald wanted that, too. To smell fresh, to feel seen, to walk into class and not feel like the village was still clinging to his skin.

He never stole it. He used leftover coins, threw away the receipt, and kept the can hidden. But no scent could hide from a mother's nose. She would ask, gently but firmly, "Where did you get this?" And though she hadn't accused him, Reginald always told the truth. Lying felt heavier than the guilt of spending a few coins. It wasn't stealing. It was survival of self-esteem. A teenager's need, not for approval, but dignity.

School in the city was different in shape but not in spirit. The walk was still long, the subjects still difficult. But being a teenager brought new trials that even his grandmother's wisdom hadn't prepared him for. There was bullying— one boy, older than the rest, taller and darker and far too comfortable in his own power, made Reginald's days heavier. He wasn't violent, but his authority was evident through his control. He ordered Reginald to run errands, buy food, and bring water. Not as a friend. Not to share. Just to remind everyone that he could.

Reginald did what he was told, not out of fear, but out of exhaustion. Resistance took energy, and energy was already being used up at home. He even did the boy's homework sometimes, his own dignity swallowed for the sake of peace. He never told his mother. Never told a teacher. Some things just become part of life, like uneven sidewalks or flickering lights. You notice them, but you learn to walk around them.

Still, the journey home each day offered a kind of healing. He walked back with friends, boys who talked too loudly and laughed too hard, sharing jokes that weren't always funny but were always warm. Sometimes they passed other children; kids with bicycles, clean shoes, games they didn't have to invent. Some were already gambling, flipping coins, and betting sweets or coins. Reginald never joined. Not because he didn't want to, but because he couldn't. He didn't have the money, and more than that, he didn't want to lose something he hadn't even owned.

So he played the games that asked only for breath and heart. Soccer on gravel. Races down alleys. Chasing shadows until the sky turned orange and the streetlights blinked awake.

And when he got home, he stepped into the same routine of washing, cleaning, preparing, checking on his siblings until the city outside grew quiet again.

In those days, he was learning more than school could ever teach. He was learning how to carry responsibility without complaint. How to guard small joys. How to survive the kind of pressure that didn't come from teachers or fists, but from expectation.

He was still young. Still learning. But already, there was a hidden strength forming beneath his silence. One who knew hardship not as punishment, but as preparation.

Moving Up

The man in the suit, sitting in his study, waiting for dinner, felt a nerve twitch at the thought of the word *punishment*.

Corporal punishment still lingered in city schools like a leftover ghost from a time nobody dared name. Though the law had already spoken against it, teachers clung to their sticks as if letting go would unravel the last threads of authority they believed they still had. Some used bamboo rods, others wielded plastic pipes that hissed through the air before striking small hands or legs. The pain was sharp, sometimes lasting, but strangely familiar. Reginald and his classmates got used to it, just as they'd gotten used to waking early, walking far, and listening more than they spoke.

But beneath the discipline and daily routines, the real battle was academic. Reginald had no one to help him with schoolwork at home; no older sibling to revise with, no parent fluent in algebra or poetry. His mother had her own burdens, and his stepfather's voice belonged more to the mines than to multiplication tables. What Reginald did have, however, was the library.

It sat just ten minutes away from the house, modest in size but filled with a quiet that welcomed him like an old friend. The books didn't speak his language at first, but they didn't mock him either. They simply waited on wooden shelves, under buzzing fluorescent lights. He went there as often as he could, borrowing what was available, reading what he could understand, and guessing what he couldn't. The textbooks his teachers referred to in class were beyond his reach, but the library filled the gaps with borrowed time and silent persistence.

He couldn't visit every day. His life was braided with chores—cleaning, cooking, laundry, minding his siblings, and the hours dissolved quickly between duty and fatigue. Still, he returned when he could, drawn by the possibility that something in those pages might make his path clearer.

Evenings were their own kind of education. As twilight painted the township in muted tones, Reginald would sometimes gather with the neighborhood boys, boys who, like him, were learning to navigate adolescence without a map. Some smoked. Some sipped from cheap bottles they had stolen or borrowed from older brothers.

Reginald never joined. Not because he thought himself better, but because something in him had already decided what kind of man he didn't want to become.

He never judged them. He understood. The smoke was warmth. The alcohol was escape. And on those cold winter nights when they lit old tires on fire, black smoke rising into an indifferent sky, it wasn't about pollution, it was about comfort. The fire didn't ask questions. It just offered heat. Around it, the boys talked about football, or girls, or dreams too far to name. Most of it was nonsense. But it made the night bearable.

Back at home, even leisure had rules. The family had one television, kept in the main house, while Reginald stayed in a separate room on the same property. Watching a show often meant asking for permission, and even when granted, the moments never stretched far. By the time he was allowed to relax, his eyes were already half-closed. Sleep came early, pulled in by exhaustion. Even on weekends, when the rules were looser, his body betrayed him. He'd fall asleep before the movie reached its climax, curled up on a stiff couch that remembered every spine that had ever leaned into it.

Freedom was not a word he knew intimately. It wasn't withheld from him cruelly, but it was rationed. Measured. Parents of that time didn't believe in giving space; they believed in shaping children the way iron was shaped—by fire, pressure, and discipline. There was love, but not always room to breathe.

Weekends, though less structured than school days, brought their own kind of burden. Reginald was expected to clean, to revise, to prepare for the week ahead. But outside, the township whispered another invitation. Other kids were louder and freer. They would make plans to roam, to wander, to escape. Sometimes they walked miles just to sit in a neighbor's lounge and watch bootleg DVDs all day. Nobody had money, but somehow, someone always had a loaf of bread or a greasy brown paper bag filled with fat cakes. The one who bought shared with the rest. It was an unspoken rule.

Moving Up

They returned home tired, sweaty, and unwashed. Sometimes in the same clothes from the day before, sometimes barefoot from losing a shoe in some ditch or muddy shortcut. Reginald often returned to the sting of reprimand and a sharp look from his mother. On rare occasions when his mother already had a bad day, a wooden spoon that cracked more pride than skin would accompany the reprimand. But still, he was resilient. He went again next time. Not out of defiance. But because he was young. And that was their version of joy. As much as his grandmother taught him discipline, she also reminded him to enjoy whatever he could at his age.

And he wanted to share as much joy as he could with his friends. It wasn't always clean, or structured, or safe. But it was theirs.

Sometimes, Reginald and his friends would go to town to raise money, not with plans, but with hope tucked into their back pockets. They had no job offers, no permits, no appointments, just open hands and open eyes. On some days, they would wash parked cars without asking. Just water, old rags, and effort. If the car owner smiled and dropped a coin into a palm, that was a good day. If they shouted, waved them off, or cursed, it wasn't surprising. They didn't protest. They simply moved on to the next dusty windshield, to the next small chance.

The streets taught lessons school never could. The streets reminded him how different people's lives could be. Reginald remembered the first time he stood near a Spur restaurant. The smell of food hit him before the sign did—steak, grilled meat, spices he couldn't name. People laughed over shiny tables, wiping sauce off their fingers with napkins they didn't need to save. Waiters walked with practiced grace, carrying plates stacked with food.

Reginald stood behind the glass. Not as a customer. Not even as a beggar. Just as a boy trying to understand how such a world could exist so close to his and yet feel galaxies away. He had never tasted a burger. Had only heard about it in passing, like a story from another country. Once, he saw someone toss half a burger into the bin, and he stood there longer than he meant to, staring not at the waste but at the question—how could life be this different? Experiences like these made him revise every lesson his grandmother taught him about life: to save, to conserve, to recycle, to create something out of nothing.

The best he and his friends could manage, if luck was kind and coins were found, were hot chips and plain bread. Not every week. Maybe once a month. It tasted like gold when it came, wrapped in greasy paper and shared with joy on a dusty curb.

That season of his life, those long, uncertain teenage years, became the beginning of an inward shift. Young Reginald started spending more time alone, not because he disliked people, but because he was beginning to notice the patterns inside his mind. He started spending more time with books than people. Isolated himself when the noise grew too loud. But, he wasn't lonely. His mind had become a room he didn't mind being in.

There was an old stereo cassette player in his room, slightly broken at the corners, but still alive in the ways that mattered. He would sit beside it late into the evening, listening to radio songs, waiting for the ones he loved. When the beat started, he would hit the record button, careful not to breathe too loudly. He had whole cassettes filled with partial songs, DJ chatter cutting into the chorus, or endings clipped too short. Still, it made him feel connected to something distant, yet real.

Sometimes he would be late for school just to finish recording a song. It didn't feel wrong. It felt necessary. Music was one of the few things in his life that didn't require permission. It was his.

Secondary school brought new faces and new challenges. Among them, he met Lawrence, a boy with clear speaking skills and a purpose even clearer. He spoke English and Afrikaans with the kind of confidence that made teachers listen. Reginald admired him quietly at first. He was very much impressed and a little scared. Then, with time, they became friends.

Lawrence was the first peer who didn't laugh at dreams. He encouraged Reginald to study harder, to read more carefully, to believe that his mind was not limited by his surroundings. Together with two others, they formed a study group. They stayed late after school, going over lessons, testing each other, sharing notes, and eating leftover bread. They did not have tutors or new textbooks. They had chalk, worn chairs, and determination.

Reginald's mind began to sharpen, not like a knife, but like a tool. He became more patient, steady, and precise. He found joy in studying. Not because it was easy, but because it made his world feel larger.

Lawrence became a kind of compass. At home, no one spoke of university. No one asked about his marks. But Lawrence did. He reminded Reginald that it was okay to want more. That dreaming of a future outside their township was not foolish, that it might even be possible.

When school ended, the group splintered. Lawrence and the others moved on, accepted into universities, their futures already taking shape in a new direction. Reginald stayed behind, not because he was a failure, but by force.

His grandparents had promised that if he did well in school, they would send him to the University of Johannesburg. And he had done well. He had the grades, the certificates, the hunger.

But nothing came.

No letters. No tickets. No explanation.

And Reginald, for reasons he still could not fully explain, never asked why.

He folded the hope quietly, tucked it into a corner of himself, and said nothing. Not because he didn't care. But because he had already learned something about disappointment, that sometimes it doesn't come with thunder or rage, sometimes, it just sits quietly at the table, waiting for you to notice its presence.

Dinner was ready. He heard a voice call out his name from the kitchen. The older Reginald went to his bedroom and took a bath. He got out fresh and clean, brushed his gray, thinning hair, and went to the dining room. He sat before everyone, even before the food was served. He had become a strong man of discipline. He respected the food he earned through hardship and the family he raised with the same love he had received from his grandma.

Reginald never ate much. He was never used to it. So after a short, quick meal, he went for a walk on the street outside his house. While taking slow and soundless steps, his mind went back to the disappointment he had felt when his grandparents did not fund his university education. The ghost of disappointment had struck him once before, when he had disappointed his stepfather.

It was the last year of school. It should have been a celebration. For most students, it was. A time of relief, of promises made beneath schoolyard trees, of stolen smiles and well-worn uniforms buttoned up for the final time. But for Reginald, the ending came with a crack—not in the sky, but across his cheek.

One night, he had gone out with friends, nothing wild, nothing reckless, just a walk through the township streets, a few laughs under the flickering streetlights, the sound of distant music carried on the wind. They sat on concrete steps and talked about life after school. About jobs, about dreams. Time slipped through their fingers like loose sand. Before he knew it, the night had become morning.

He returned home quietly, only to find the door to his small room swinging open. He had forgotten to lock it. His stepfather was already awake, pacing, his voice gruff with worry and frustration. The conversation started with questions. Where were you? What were you thinking? —and ended with something Reginald had never experienced before.

A slap.

Just once. But it landed with more than force.

It landed with finality.

Reginald did not shout or cry. He did not explain how the night had passed harmlessly, how there had been no drinking, no girls, no crimes, just time moving too fast, and boys talking too long.

But he didn't say any of it. Because in that moment, the slap said enough.

It said, *I don't trust you.*

It said, *You are not safe in your own home*

Moving Up

It said, *Whatever you've carried, whatever you've survived, still counts for nothing.*

So, without ceremony, Reginald left.

He packed a small bag and walked out that same day. No fights, no letters. Just absence.

He caught a ride to his uncle's place in the Northwest, arriving just before the holidays began. Nobody asked why he had come early. He didn't volunteer the truth. Instead, he smiled and shrugged and said something vague about school ending soon. That bought him time. He slept well those first few nights, not because things were better, but because he was tired of pretending.

When the holidays ended, Reginald didn't return to the city. He didn't return to school. He went instead to the village, a different one this time. And there, life began to change again, but not in the way he had once dreamed.

His older cousin welcomed him with the kind of grin that suggested freedom. No alarms. No chores. No expectations.

There, Reginald entered a new chapter, one marked not by study sessions or library books, but by taverns and bottle caps.

At first, he watched. The cousin drank easily, daily, like water. He was already out of school, already indifferent. Reginald hesitated. He was still a boy who remembered exams, still a boy who feared girls. But the cousin laughed loud, bought drinks with borrowed coins, and made recklessness seem like ritual.

Reginald tried his first real drink there. It burned his throat, not just with heat but with shame. He felt something dull inside him. But he didn't stop. The days became a blur of late mornings and hazy evenings, of taverns filled with stories told too loudly and promises forgotten before sunrise.

That season didn't last long. But it left its mark.

Looking back, he would call it *a quick, dirty education*—the kind of learning no textbook could offer. He saw what carelessness could become. He saw how boys with no plan became men with no peace.

There were still small reminders of who he really was. Reminders that flickered even in the smoke-filled rooms.

When his school celebrated the end of the academic year, Reginald had nothing to wear. He hadn't planned for it. He hadn't imagined he'd still be part of it. His mother's sister stepped in, quietly, without fuss. She handed him a blazer. It was borrowed, a little too big, and completely mismatched with his trousers. But it was something.

He wore it proudly. Not because he looked good, but because he had made it that far.

One teacher, who had been trying to find him for weeks, finally did. She showed up unexpectedly, her eyes wide with relief and reproach. She didn't yell. She didn't scold. She simply sat beside him on a bench and said,

"You are too smart to disappear like this."

He looked away, not because he disagreed, but because he wasn't used to hearing it.

"You know," she added, softer now, "potential is a gift, but it's not permanent. If you leave it alone, it leaves you too."

Her words stayed with him.

His school results were good. Not the best, but close. Good enough to open doors, had there been someone to turn the handle. People knew his name. Some still spoke it with respect, as if it meant something more than just a record in a register.

Everything he had achieved, he had done without tutors, without home support, without promises of reward. He had friends like Lawrence and Abby. He had a mind that refused to give up. And sometimes, he had teachers who reminded him of his worth.

But what he didn't have was a next step.

Moving Up

His grandparents had once told him, "Do well, and we'll send you to university in Johannesburg." He had done his part. But the rest never came.

No train ticket. No phone call. No explanation.

And Reginald, as he had always done, kept his silence.

He never asked why. Not because he didn't want answers, but because he had already learned that not all questions find their way home.

He spent those days wandering through thoughts more than places. Some mornings he'd sit outside with an old newspaper and try to sound out every word. Some nights he'd lie in bed, headphones on, listening to songs that felt like they were written just for him. He'd read quotes from books he couldn't afford to own, scribbling them on bits of paper, tucking them into the lining of his wallet or under his mattress.

One of his favorites was this:

"Education is the most powerful weapon which you can use to change the world."

– Nelson Mandela

He didn't just copy it, he believed it even when the world around him gave him no map, even when the school gates felt too far behind him. Even when all he had was borrowed clothes and borrowed time.

Reginald was no longer a boy. Not quite a man. But something was building in him—resistance, shaped by disappointment and lit by memory.

He didn't know what would come next.

But he knew who he didn't want to become.

And sometimes, that's the beginning of everything.

Chapter 4: Grandmother's love and loss

There was no ceremony the day Reginald stepped into adulthood. No speech. No handshake. No photograph to mark the moment. Just a slow morning in the village, the clatter of a tin cup on the floor, and the sudden realization that he was now the only one left at home.

After completing his high school, he decided to go back to his village. The reason? To bond with his father, his biological father. But the day he reached, he did not know that all his plans and efforts were going to go in vain. His father had gone to Johannesburg. Said he needed a change of air. Claimed he had to visit his mother and sister. But Reginald understood better than most—his father wasn't running toward anything; he was running away. Away from the stillness of the village, the kind that echoes after harvest season and makes a man question the sound of his own breath. He had left Reginald the house, the keys, the walls, and the weight.

For nearly two months, it was just him.

Him and the echo of footsteps that never returned. Him and the silence that moved from one room to another. Him and the humble meals he learned to prepare with whatever coins clinked in his pocket. The house didn't run itself. The chores didn't call his name. But they were his now. Unapologetically his.

He was seventeen. Still wet with the dust of childhood but already crusted with the weight of manhood. And manhood didn't arrive with fireworks. It slipped in quietly, through the cracks of a half-opened door, while no one was looking.

Reginald learned quickly. He learned how long maize meal lasted, how much water to boil, how to ration salt. He learned that socks stiffen when they dry too long under a hot sun. He learned that hunger doesn't ask questions, it just waits in silence.

He had returned home hoping to bond with his father. Instead, he was handed an empty house and the task of surviving it.

And then, life began throwing lemons.

Moving Up

Not the kind you squeeze into cold drinks. The kind that land heavy in your lap at dusk. The kind that bruise your pride and don't come with instructions.

He wanted to study. To continue his education. But the door of learning that once stood wide open was already closing before he could step through it. There were no funds, no scholarships, no maps showing what to do next. There was just Reginald, standing on the edge of a dream that didn't know his name.

So he did the only thing a dreamless boy could do—he looked for work.

Not work that had titles or desks. Not the kind of work that smelled of leather shoes and polished corridors. He looked for work that bit at the knuckles and tore at the skin. General labor. The one job that asked no questions but demanded everything in return.

He knocked on doors with empty hands and a willing spirit. Told men he could lift, dig, clean, do whatever was needed. One finally said yes.

That "yes" introduced him to cement, bricks, aching joints, and dust that nested deep in his lungs. The job became his teacher. It taught him survival and the slow ache of tired feet. He did it without complaint, because there was no one to complain to.

He stayed in that labor for over a year.

And when the contract ended, he didn't return home. Instead, he drifted further, to another province, where he believed hope might wear overalls and carry a shovel. He followed the whisper of work near the mines—not to dig, but to find something on the fringes. Anything that resembled opportunity.

That's when the call came.

His grandmother was sick.

Fatally sick. With the kind of illness that silences rooms and softens footsteps. She had been the core of his world—the only maternal figure he had fully known. The one who taught him to boil water, fold prayers, and fight off storms with humility.

He missed her final week. Missed her final story. He received the news like a whisper too cold for the ear. He rushed home—bags unpacked, plans discarded. He missed her final week. Missed her final story. He arrived just before they laid her down. Just in time to see the village women circle the grave, dust slipping through their fingers. Just in time to kneel beside the mound and whisper something only she would understand. Arrived just in time to see the hem of her blanket disappear beneath the earth.

It hit him later, when the world resumed its orbit – it never stopped for anyone, and he stood outside in the stillness. That's when it came, like a wave that had held its breath too long. The pain of knowing he had lost the one person who had ever looked at him with eyes that said *you are enough.*

She had been his pillar. The kind of woman whose love didn't need to be loud, rather, it lived in the small things: warm porridge, heartfelt prayers, and the way her hand lingered a little longer on his shoulder when she walked past.

With her gone, something fundamental shifted.

The village, once held together by her presence, now felt hollow. Her death wasn't just a personal loss; it was a crumbling of the only safe space he had known. There was no more reason to stay. The house still stood, the trees still rustled, but the warmth was gone.

Grief didn't scream. It sat beside him like a shadow on the bus ride home. It was silent, heavy, and unshakeable. He tried to settle again in the village, but it no longer spoke his language. The soil, the air, the trees—they were all the same, but Reginald was not.

The village had raised him. But it could no longer contain him. It no longer gave him a sense of belonging.

So Reginald did what he always did when life took something from him—he left.

No job. No plan. Just a thin thread of hope from his uncle, his mother's younger brother, who had said over the phone, "Come, I've got something for you." He hadn't mentioned what.

Reginald arrived and was handed a uniform and a role: security guard.

That first night, winter greeted him with open arms. Cold crept into his bones through the seams of his jacket. He stood outside a nondescript building in a part of town that had long forgotten kindness. The streetlights flickered uncertainly, and somewhere nearby, dogs barked like sentinels of a darker truth. Reginald gripped his flashlight, unsure whether he was guarding the building or guarding himself from it.

There was no shelter, no introduction, no easing in. Just hours of silence and shadow.

But he endured it.

Because that was the only thing he knew how to do—endure.

Every ache in his legs, every frozen breath, every passing stranger who looked at him without really seeing him—it all became part of the initiation, not into the job, but into the deeper understanding of what it meant to survive when the world offered nothing but necessity.

He worked like that for weeks. Night after night, the same routine. Stand. Watch. Wait.

There were no breaks. Only fatigue that folded into habit. He didn't complain—not to his uncle, not to the wind, not even to himself. Complaint was a luxury for people who believed things could change.

But he stood his post. Because when hunger is your closest companion, dignity becomes quite a luxury.

And then, like a cracked window finally letting in light, a stranger changed everything.

Michael Hollenstien. Swiss-German. The owner of the hotel, Reginald, had been posted outside.

He looked at Reginald with interest and keen curiosity.

"You don't belong out here," he said.

He invited him inside.

And that, without ceremony or trumpet, became the turning point.

The man looked him over. Not with disdain, but with a kind of curious evaluation.

"What's your name?"

"Reginald, sir."

"You don't belong out here," the man said, almost to himself.

Reginald wasn't sure what that meant. He stood still.

"You ever worked in hospitality?"

"No, sir."

"Ever been a waiter?"

He shook his head.

The man nodded. "Come inside tomorrow. Ask for me—Michael Hollenstien."

And just like that, the map shifted.

The next day, Reginald showed up—still in uniform, unsure whether this had been a real offer or just a passing comment from a man with too many opinions and too much money. But Michael remembered. He welcomed him in, offered him a plain shirt, and told him to start with the windows.

And so Reginald did.

He didn't start as a waiter. He started with a rag and a bucket, washing hotel windows from the outside, exposed to the same cold that had kept him company as a guard. It was thankless work—tedious, repetitive, and physically demanding. The first week, there were four of them assigned to the windows. By the second week, only two remained. One had quit mid-shift, muttering something about dignity. The other had simply disappeared.

Reginald stayed.

Not because he enjoyed the work, but because he understood what it meant to begin at the bottom. He didn't resent it. He studied it. Every smudge he wiped away taught him something. Every comment from staff, whether mocking or indifferent, sharpened him. He wasn't there to be liked. He was there to learn.

And he learned quickly.

He noticed the way the place worked. His eyes moved with the way the waiters moved between tables, how they greeted guests, and how the kitchen staff communicated in a flurry of clicks and commands. He paid attention to the hierarchy, the habits, the rituals.

He began to want in—not just physically, but mentally. To step beyond the windows and become part of the scene inside.

But he was patient. Because patience was the one thing life had taught him thoroughly.

Michael noticed. Perhaps he saw in Reginald a version of himself—a younger man, shaped by adversity but not defined by it.

Slowly, he brought him in.

First to sweep floors, then to carry trays. And eventually, to shadow a senior waiter.

It wasn't glamorous. But it was something.

Reginald stood straighter with each shift. He memorized the menu. Learned how to pour wine without spilling a drop. He practiced his English in front of a cracked mirror at night. He paid attention to posture, tone, timing.

And all the while, something began to shift inside him.

He wasn't just working.

He was building.

A sense of self. A sense of direction. A future that, for the first time, didn't feel borrowed or forced.

Each tip he received went toward a goal he hadn't yet spoken aloud: to study again. To go back to school, not for anyone else, but for himself. And though the hours were long, and the nights still cold, the hope that had once felt so distant was now something he could almost touch.

In that hotel, among clinking glasses and passing plates, Reginald began to rewrite his story.

Not as a victim of circumstance, but as a young man with dust on his shoes and fire in his soul.

And for the first time in a long time, he believed he might just make it.

Only the man in the suit knew the truth. Oh, how far he had made it. And how much he was proud of himself for persevering. he was enjoying the fruit of the hard work that younger Reginald did.

Once the rhythm of hotel work had steadied, Reginald did something most men in his shoes would have postponed—he enrolled in college.

It wasn't a grand moment. There was no fanfare, no applause, no one clapping him on the back. Just a fileld registration form, a crumpled receipt, and the heavy awareness that every rand he spent on tuition was a rand not spent on food or transport.

But he signed the papers anyway.

He hadn't forgotten his dream. The dream that had flickered faintly even when he was carrying bricks, even when his socks stiffened in the village sun, even when his grandmother's blanket had been lowered into the earth. Education had always been the unlit torch he carried close to his chest.

He was waiting for the right spark, and the hotel job provided that spark.

His income was modest. Tips, the occasional raise, careful budgeting, but it was enough. Enough to shape a new path. Enough to start. And that was all he needed.

Reginald began taking classes on his off days. It was a delicate dance—balancing the demands of hotel service with the rigor of academics. His life reduced itself into three strict categories: work, study, and sleep. There was no time for socializing, no time for leisure. Just a series of early mornings and late nights, each stitched together by determination.

His room was small and barely wide enough for a mattress. It contained a stack of worn notebooks, and the secondhand textbooks he bought with careful calculation. It wasn't comfort that drove him. It was purpose.

But not everyone around him shared that purpose.

There were colleagues, some older, some his age, who treated his efforts with insolent mockery. They whispered when he walked past, made offhand remarks about him "trying too hard," or laughed behind his back when he rushed out in his uniform to catch a ride to college. Some called him arrogant, others naïve. A few even tried to convince him to quit.

"You think a piece of paper will change your life?" one sneered, towel slung lazily over his shoulder in the staff room. "We've all got dreams, my guy. Doesn't mean they pay the bills."

But Reginald didn't flinch.

He had seen worse than mockery. He had buried worse. If anything, their doubt became fuel. His goal wasn't to impress anyone, it was to become someone he himself could respect.

So he pressed on.

The commute to college was brutal. He had no car, no motorbike, not even a bicycle. He relied on hitchhiking, standing by the roadside in the predawn chill, his breath rising in thin clouds, thumb extended, waiting for a stranger with a spare seat.

Some days, he'd catch a ride quickly. Other days, he'd walk part of the distance before anyone stopped.

It was a two-hour journey each way. There and back.

And even then, the road was only the beginning.

The lectures were intense. He was older than some of his classmates, more tired than most, and often the only one juggling a full-time job with coursework. But he listened closely, took notes like his life depended on it—because in many ways, it did. He didn't have the luxury of failing. Every test, every assignment, every attendance mark was an act of defiance against the life that had tried to script him otherwise.

At night, he would return to his room, eat whatever he could afford. Often it was just bread and tea. He would then review his notes by the light of a single lamp. The hotel shifts would follow, early and unrelenting. But he adapted. He carved focus out of fatigue. Patience had become his greatest muscle, and he flexed it daily.

Then, slowly, the results began to show.

Assignments came back with high marks. Lecturers began to call him by name. Concepts that had once seemed like riddles now made sense. It wasn't just academic success, it was a new way of thinking. A new vision of who he could be.

And all of it, Reginald knew, stemmed from one moment.

That conversation with Michael Hollenstien.

The man who had seen him not as a guard, but as something more. The man who had handed him opportunity like a candle in the dark and trusted him to carry it forward.

Michael hadn't micromanaged him. He hadn't hovered or overpraised. But he had opened the door. That was enough. Sometimes, all someone needs is a door that doesn't slam shut on sight.

Reginald didn't take that for granted.

Moving Up

He showed up on time. Stayed late when needed. Took every task seriously, from sweeping floors to carrying trays. And Michael noticed. Promotions came—not grand, but steady. First, to the barman. Then, to roles with more responsibility, more trust. Raises followed, sometimes quiet, private acknowledgments from the top, gestures that said: "I see you. Keep going."

And he did.

He worked hard. Studied harder. And, when the occasion called, played hard too—because life, in its fragile brilliance, had finally given him a chance, and he intended to live it fully.

Still, the isolation never completely left him.

Family remained distant. His father was a blurred figure, orbiting the edge of his life. His mother, further still, unreachable not by distance, but by memory. The village? A place he visited only when necessary. It still held ghosts. It still held shadows. He hadn't healed entirely, and perhaps he never would. But he had learned to live with the wound. To move despite it.

Reginald had come a long way from the boy left alone in a rural house with no instructions. He was no longer just surviving. He was building. Brick by brick, lesson by lesson.

And though he hadn't set out to become a hotelier, the industry had wrapped itself around him. It had given him structure, identity, and a kind of belonging. Over time, it became more than a job. It became a craft.

He understood now that dreams don't always look the way you imagine them. Sometimes, they arrive wearing different clothes, speaking different languages. But if you're open and if you're brave, they still take you where you're meant to go.

And Reginald was going.

However, it wasn't supposed to end the way it did.

One heated exchange. One moment where pride and fatigue collided. A misunderstanding with a supervisor, which was minor in scale but major in consequence. Words were exchanged, tempers rose, and Reginald made a decision he would later reflect on with mixed emotions.

He quit.

No notice. No backup plan. Just a bag slung over his shoulder and a slow walk out of the hotel that had become more than just a workplace. For the first time in years, he stepped into uncertainty, not because life had forced it, but because he had chosen it.

With nowhere else to go, he boarded a bus to Johannesburg.

He didn't call ahead. He didn't ask for permission. He simply arrived, dusty, disoriented, and unannounced.

When his grandfather opened the door, the expression on his face said everything.

"What are you doing here?" the old man asked, not cruelly, but sharply. "This is Johannesburg. You don't just show up."

Reginald tried to explain. Tried to soften the reality of why he'd left. But the words didn't land. His grandfather was old-school—he believed in protocol, in responsibility, in respecting the boundaries of adulthood.

"You could have been killed," he muttered, voice gravelly with worry and judgment. "This city isn't forgiving. Don't ever arrive like this again."

Reginald nodded, apologized, and quietly moved into the spare room. For the next few weeks, he did nothing. No work. No school. No direction. He drifted around the house like a guest overstaying his welcome, watching the days pass through half-closed curtains.

For the first time in a long time, he felt still—and not the peaceful kind.

But life, in its strange choreography, had not forgotten him.

One evening, as he sat staring out at the city's gold-lit skyline, his phone rang.

The name on the screen made his heart jolt: *Michael Hollenstien.*

He answered quickly.

"Reginald," the voice said. Calm. Clear. Familiar. "What happened?"

Reginald exhaled. Explained. Not with excuses, but with honesty. Told Michael about the misunderstanding, the impulse to leave, and the uncertainty that followed.

There was a pause on the other end.

Then: "Come back. Let's sort it out. These are internal issues, and they don't define you."

It wasn't a demand. It was an invitation. The same kind of invitation he'd received that first time outside the hotel doors.

The next morning, Reginald returned.

Michael was waiting for him, not with anger or reprimand, but with something more powerful: belief.

"We all make mistakes," he said. "What matters is how we return from them."

Reginald promised to give it his all. And he did.

He came back with new humility, new fire. He didn't just *want* to do better, he *needed* to. For himself, for the future he'd started to build with bare hands and tired feet.

He started again as a waiter, but not for long.

The floor manager noticed his precision. The guests remembered his name. He moved with confidence and spoke with clarity. And before long, he was promoted to barman.

It was a role that suited him.

The bar was always in motion. An orchestrated chaos that required both grace and grit. Reginald found his flow behind the counter. He learned drink recipes like poetry, remembered customer preferences like personal secrets, and handled rush hours with the composure of someone who had known deeper struggles.

From there, life began to reward his persistence.

Each year brought something good. Sometimes, it was a new responsibility. Other times, a raise. Occasionally, both.

The CEO, normally a distant figure in a tailored suit, took a personal interest in Reginald. He called him into his office once, offered him a raise quietly, outside the cycle of company-wide adjustments.

"I've seen your work," he said. "This is just a thank you."

Moments like that fueled him.

It wasn't the money, it was the recognition. The subtle confirmation that his presence mattered. That his effort wasn't invisible.

Reginald didn't waste the money either. He was careful. Strategic. But he also allowed himself small joys. A good meal here. A modest pair of shoes there. Nights out where he could laugh freely, dance without worry. He had learned to work hard, and study harder, and somehow, amidst the long hours, the clinking glasses, the whispers of doubt and approval, he had built a life.

It wasn't the life he had imagined as a child staring out of village windows.

But it was a life shaped by resilience, earned inch by inch, through mistakes and mercy.

And it was his.

Despite his progress, despite the balance he had finally found between work and study, the cracks in Reginald's past had never fully closed. Especially not where family was concerned.

The ties that were supposed to hold him, the ones woven by blood and birth, had frayed over time. Some had snapped entirely. His relationship with his father was distant, more like memory than presence. There were no phone calls. No questions. Just a familiar absence that Reginald no longer questioned.

His mother? That chapter had closed long before he understood how pages turn. Whatever tenderness had once existed between them had been buried beneath an unspoken something. Something unresolved.

He never talked about it. Not to friends. Not even to himself in the quiet hours. But it hovered, an ache just under the ribs. A scar so old it had become part of his posture.

Finding his own way had never been a choice. It had been a necessity.

But in doing so, in walking alone through all the uncertainty and dirt and night shifts and lecture halls, he had found something more valuable than acceptance: he had found himself.

It was ironic, really, how life never gave him what he asked for. No stable household. No doting parents. No gentle guidance. Instead, life handed him the opposite. Rejection. Loss. Hardship. Delay.

And yet... that very opposition became the soil in which a new dream grew.

He had stopped expecting life to offer comfort. Instead, he learned how to carve meaning from chaos. How to build a structure from silence. He had learned how to belong to himself.

Once a year, he still returned to the village. Not for nostalgia. Not for closure. Just because it was the only place that had ever loosely resembled home. But even then, his visits were brief. He never unpacked fully. He kept one foot by the door.

As for his mother's place, he hadn't set foot there in over two decades.

There had been an incident. One that had quietly redrawn the borders of his emotional landscape. He never spoke about it. And if someone asked, he would shrug it off, as if it were too distant to recall clearly. But he remembered. Every detail. Every silence that followed.

Healing never came. Not fully.

If someone asked him whether he had forgiven, he wouldn't know what to say. He didn't hate anyone—not directly, not intentionally. But he *did* hate the place. The soil. The walls. The smell of memory lingered in every room.

That place didn't just hold bad moments, it breathed them.

Sure, if he really tried, he could zoom in and find the good. A joke shared. A meal eaten on the floor. A cousin's laughter echoed down a dusty path. But those moments were blurred, outnumbered. The pain was sharper. More defined.

He didn't know if he'd ever go back.

Maybe one day, older, wiser, less afraid. Maybe then he could stand there, not as a son returning, but as a man confronting a ghost.

But not now.

No one else held that picture. Only he knew the version of that house that haunted him. The version others romanticized, he remembered it differently. More jagged. Less forgiving.

There were still people from that past he cared about. A few he kept in touch with occasional phone calls, messages passed through mutual relatives. But he never shared his full story with them. Never told them what he had become. Or what he had survived.

Especially not those who once tried to lead him down paths he refused to take.

He remembered them, too. The ones who tempted him with shortcuts, with shadows, with small-time rebellion. He had walked away from all of it. But he still carried the tension in his spine.

He wasn't sure why he hadn't fully healed.

Maybe because healing requires confrontation, and he had never gone back to confront what had hurt him. He had ignored it, tucked it deep into the folds of his growing success.

But ignoring isn't the same as forgetting.

Moving Up

He often felt like he was still living with the shadow of that place. It didn't affect his choices. It didn't steer his days. But it was there, watching from a distance.

Sometimes, he thought of it as a sleeping beast, curled in the attic of his subconscious. Dormant, but never dead.

He knew one day, he'd have to wake it.

Gently. Carefully. And set it free.

He didn't know when that day would come, maybe when he had children of his own. Maybe when his voice no longer trembled at the thought of his mother's name. Maybe when forgiveness felt like strength, not surrender.

But it would come.

Until then, he moved forward quietly, carrying both the dream he had built and the history he had buried.

Chapter 5: First Love, First Heartbreak

Long before Reginald learned how to balance wine glasses and memorize guest orders, long before Johannesburg's skyline etched itself into his memory, there was a girl. Not just any girl. The first one.

Elizabeth came into his life quietly, without ceremony. There was no grand entrance, no warning. Just a smile across the schoolyard and a conversation that lingered longer than it should have. At the time, Reginald didn't know what love was. Not in the way poets wrote about it, or how films made it look. But he knew what it felt like to wait by the corner of a house for someone to show up. And he knew what it meant when they didn't.

Lizzy was his high school girlfriend and his first real relationship. The kind of love that sneaks up on you when you're too young to know how to protect your heart. And because it was first, it was everything. Reginald, still wrapped in the fragile skin of adolescence, loved her with the full weight of someone who didn't yet understand what love could cost.

They had a place. A small patch of world behind her house, tucked away from curious eyes and disapproving parents. It wasn't much, just a dusty corner with a view of the sky, but to them, it was sacred. They'd meet there whenever they could. No phones. No text messages. Just timing, intuition, and the hope that she'd be there.

Sometimes, she was. Sometimes, she wasn't.

And that uncertainty became the beginning of the unraveling.

After school ended, Reginald left town briefly to visit family in the village. It wasn't meant to be long. Just a visit. A pause. But when he returned, something had shifted. The air between them wasn't the same. Her gaze no longer lingered. Her silence spoke louder than anything she could have said.

Still, he showed up. Faithful. Hopeful. Oblivious.

Moving Up

He'd wait at the usual spot, sometimes alone, sometimes with his friend Willie. Even in the dead cold of winter, he'd stand there, scanning the house, willing her to appear. And on one of those nights with numb fingers, breath hanging in the air, she did. Briefly. She stepped out, saw him, and slipped back inside like a shadow.

No wave. No smile. No explanation.

It was the kind of silence that fills you up, not with peace, but with questions.

He kept going back. Night after night. Until the truth arrived, not from her, but from whispers. Friends. Fragments of gossip strung together into something that began to make sense.

Lizzy had moved on. Found someone else. Someone who was older, employed and present. Someone she deserved.

Reginald had only his love to offer. And it turned out, that wasn't enough.

He broke quietly. No dramatic outburst. No angry words. Just withdrawal. Isolation. The slow folding of a heart that had opened too quickly. He stopped laughing. Stopped talking. Friends noticed. Some made jokes. Others avoided the subject altogether.

And then, months later, she walked into his home like nothing had happened. Sat across from him. Looked him in the eyes. And said she came to check if he was okay.

Lizzy had moved on, she said.

As if that was something that could be said out loud and left hanging in the room like it didn't carry weight.

Reginald didn't scream. He didn't argue. But something inside him shifted. It was the moment he realized that love could end without warning. That someone could hold your heart one day and drop it the next, without even meaning to.

He carried that pain for years. It settled quietly and deeply withing him and shaped him in ways he wouldn't fully understand until much later.

After that heartbreak, something in him hardened. He still loved, but not the same way. Not as freely. Not as blindly. The boy who once waited in the cold, believing love was enough, had become a man who measured his steps more carefully.

And yet, despite all that came after—the hotel job, the college nights, the slow climb out of obscurity—her memory lingered. Not as a regret. Not even as a wound. But as a reminder.

That the first cut is the deepest.

And some lessons never fade.

Years later, when the dust of youth had long settled and his hands had known the weight of work, the man in the suit would still think of her. Not every day. Not with pain that pierced, but with a kind of familiar heaviness. Like a scar that stopped aching but still knew how to catch the light at the wrong angle.

He had become a different man. Life had taken him far from the boy who once waited by the wall, heart full of hope and fingers numb with winter. Johannesburg had shaped him. Work had matured him. Struggle had seasoned him. But every now and then, in the quiet hours, when the world slowed, when the children were asleep, and Precious, his wife's breathing was steady beside him, his mind would wander.

Not with regret. Not with longing. But with wonder.

What would life have looked like had things not ended the way they did?

Not because he wished it differently. No, he loved his family deeply. His wife, his children; they were his anchor. But love, real love, doesn't always erase the echoes that came before. It builds over them. And some echoes, no matter how faint, still carry a voice.

He remembered returning from the village after that brief visit. How the roads seemed unfamiliar, even though nothing had changed. How the house he used to glance at with anticipation now made his chest tighten. He hadn't expected anything to be different. She had promised, after all. They had promised.

But the promises of teenagers are made with ink that washes away in the first rain.

Moving Up

What hurt most wasn't that she had moved on. It was that she had done so without a word. No explanation. No soft landing. Just absence.

He didn't know if it had started while he was away. Maybe it had always been there, hidden in the margins of their meetings. Maybe he had missed the signs. Or maybe, as often happens with young love, one person simply grows tired before the other does.

Still, he hadn't been prepared.

He would find himself retracing old steps. Walking past the places they once sat, trying to read the air for meaning. He'd go with Willie or alone, waiting near the corner, half-hoping she would appear. And when she didn't, he'd stand a little longer, as if presence alone could bring back what time had already taken.

At school, his was focus lost. Pages blurred. Lessons drifted past. His friends noticed, though few said anything. One joked that whatever kept him at the wall would be the same thing that pulled him away from it. He had laughed then—a forced, shallow laugh, but those words stayed with him longer than the joke intended.

It was hard to admit, even to himself, how deeply it had affected him.

Heartbreak at that age doesn't announce itself as trauma. It settles quietly, like dust in the corners of the mind. It teaches you things that no adult conversation ever prepares you for. How love can sharpen you or shatter you. How someone's silence can be louder than any scream. How the person who once made you feel seen can vanish, and you're left wondering if you ever existed to them at all.

Looking back now, with years layered between the boy he was and the man he became, Reginald could see it for what it was: a necessary ending. Not because it lacked feeling, but because it lacked future. They were too young, too unsure, too unready. Love, in its truest form, demands more than emotion. It needs timing. Maturity. A willingness to carry weight together.

They hadn't known how to do that. And maybe they weren't supposed to.

But still, she remained unforgettable.

Even now, her name lingered in certain memories like perfume that hadn't faded. He wouldn't say it out loud, not out of shame, but out of respect. Some names belong to quiet places. She was one of them.

She would appear to him occasionally in dreams—not as the girl she was, but as a feeling. A version of tenderness he had once known. A what-if dressed in sunlight. Not to torment him, but to remind him that love, when real, leaves a mark.

And yet, for all the sentiment, he had never wished to return to her. That chapter, painful as it was, had written something essential into his story. It had given him depth. Taught him caution. Shaped his compass.

It also taught him that not every love is meant to last. Some are simply meant to teach.

She had taught him how much of himself he was willing to give. And how easily that could be dismissed. She had taught him how to sit with emptiness. How to walk through days that didn't offer answers. How to begin again.

After she left, Reginald sat in silence for a long time.

He didn't cry. He just let the weight of it settle fully for the first time. He wouldn't see her again. Not intentionally. Not in person.

But her shadow stayed.

Not in the way that haunted him. But in the way that shaped how he approached love from that day on. He became guarded. Careful. He learned to hold parts of himself back—not out of fear, but out of instinct.

Love, he had learned, could be a thief. It could take without warning. It could leave you standing outside in the cold, holding nothing but the memory of warmth.

So, when love found him again years later, gentler, steadier—he didn't dive in. He walked. Slowly. Intentionally. But he was ready.

The woman who became his wife didn't look like the girl from high school. She didn't speak like her or laugh like her. But she held Reginald differently—from the beginning—with a kind of consistency he hadn't known before. No dramatic entrances. No disappearances.

Just presence.

And that made all the difference.

Still, even as a married man with children, Reginald could admit, if only to himself, that the first heartbreak had never fully left. It was the first time life taught him that things don't always go as planned. That people change. That love isn't always enough.

And that was okay.

Because pain, like love, has a purpose.

It wakes you up. Stretches your spirit. Reminds you that you are capable of healing—even when you think you're not.

Years later, sitting in his small home, a cup of tea in hand, he would smile at the thought—not bitter, not broken, just aware.

She had been his first.

And she had left a mark.

But he had lived, and he had grown.

The man in the suit still remembered the time he spent with that girl. She still entered his thoughts in the quietest moments. When Reginald returned from the village that final time—sunburned shoulders, mind caught between revision notes and unanswered questions—he thought he was stepping back into something familiar. The world he had left behind had only shifted by a few weeks, a month at most. Nothing should have changed. And yet, everything had.

He came back with the weight of upcoming exams resting squarely on his chest, the kind of pressure that tugs at your sleep and dulls your appetite. But even then, in the thick of academic anxiety, he still made time. Not for textbooks. Not for tutors. But for her.

They had a corner. Their "Lovers' Corner". A dusty slice of suburbia tucked away behind her house. It wasn't special to the world—just a stretch of earth with no benches, no trees, no signposts. But it had become sacred in the way that young lovers assign meaning to ordinary things. That small patch of land had held stolen moments, whispered promises, awkward laughter, and the kind of stillness that only appears when you believe time is yours to waste.

It was their meeting place. Their bubble. A hiding spot from parental eyes and noisy siblings and the slow ticking of adolescence. Sometimes, they would hold each other. Sometimes, they would just talk. But every time they met there, something quiet was built. Or at least, that's what Reginald had believed.

He hadn't noticed the cracks forming.

The first few visits after his return were unremarkable. He'd go there, sometimes alone, sometimes with a friend, usually Willie, hoping for what had always happened before: that she would appear, maybe with that half-smile she wore so casually, and they would drift into their usual swing. Nothing grand, just presence. That's all he had ever asked for—her presence. He thought they would talk to each other, cuddle maybe, and do what lovers do.

But something had shifted, almost imperceptibly.

The first time she didn't show, he didn't think much of it. Perhaps her father was home. The man was strict, protective in the way rural fathers often are. If he was around, she wouldn't risk it. Reginald understood that. He respected it.

The second time she didn't come, he told himself it was a coincidence.

By the third time, he started to feel the weight of absence in his bones.

That afternoon, he had gone with Willie. The two of them stood quietly at their usual spot, occasionally talking, mostly waiting. The sun was soft that day. Winter light filtered through dusty air, and Reginald kept glancing toward the house, hoping to catch a glimpse of movement, of her silhouette behind the curtain, of something to suggest she hadn't forgotten.

But the house remained still.

The wait stretched into evening. Willie made a few jokes, light-hearted but laced with concern, trying to fill the silence with something that didn't feel like abandonment. "Whatever put you here will take you out," he had said. Reginald smiled, thinly. The joke didn't land the way jokes should. It hovered awkwardly between them like smoke with nowhere to go.

She never came.

"Whatever put you here will take you out as well," Willie had said, and Reginald secured the words in his heart, aiming to never go back to the "Lovers' Corner".

And yet, Reginald went back again the next day. And the one after that.

It became an unspoken ritual; arriving with hope, leaving with less of it. He couldn't say exactly what he was waiting for. Maybe for her to step out and explain, even without words. Maybe for her to return to the rhythm they had created before he left. Maybe just to know he hadn't imagined it all.

But the truth was beginning to shape itself, even if he wasn't ready to say it aloud.

Love, when it's real, especially when it's your first, doesn't end with a door slammed shut. It ends slowly, in the silence between two people who used to meet at the same place. It ends in the absence that becomes routine. It ends in questions that don't get answered, because no one is left to ask them.

Reginald had been young. And young love doesn't make room for grey areas. It sees in absolutes; forever or never, all or nothing. He had believed in the fairy tale. That theirs was the kind of love that would stretch past exams, past distance, past the difficult parts that no one warns you about.

He had pictured her by his side, not just that year, but in all the years that followed. At graduations. At family weddings. Maybe even in the quiet stillness of their own small home, years from now. That was the power of that first love. It made the future look like a canvas where only one color mattered.

And so, when she stopped showing up, when her absence became the most predictable part of his day, it was like thunder on a clear afternoon—sudden, disorienting, and loud in the places where everything else had grown quiet.

He didn't confront her. He wouldn't have known how. What do you say to someone who has quietly left without leaving a note? He just kept going back, hoping, waiting, enduring.

The waiting was its own kind of heartbreak.

It stripped away his focus. His exams felt distant. His body showed up in class, but his mind stayed elsewhere, curled up behind her house, scanning the windows, searching for closure. But there was none.

Even his friends began to notice. They didn't say it outright, but they saw it in his silence, in how he no longer lingered in conversations, how he walked slower, looked down more. Willie stopped making jokes. The laughter had become too heavy to carry.

He had stopped responding to people making fun of his loneliness. People who would linger in narrow hallways and whisper, "Look, Reginald and that girl aren't together anymore."

He has simply stopped caring and he was content with the loss of emotions.

Looking back now, Reginald could see how that period shaped him more than any textbook or lecture ever did. It was the first time he had given someone his full, unfiltered self. And it was the first time that gift had gone unanswered.

Approximately three months later, when Reginald had finally begun to accept the absence, when the ache had begun to fold itself into something dull and manageable, she returned.

Not through a letter. Not through a friend. Not with explanation or apology. She simply walked into his home one afternoon, as if absence had never introduced itself between them. She stood there on the threshold of his silence, with the calm of someone who believed her presence still made sense. And maybe, in her world, it did.

Reginald remembers the air that day. Still. Thick with memory. He remembers the way her eyes swept over the room, landing on him like they used to, but without the softness that once lived there. She said, "Hi, I came to check on you, if you are okay. I just want to tell you to stop waiting for me. I have moved on, and it's time that you do too." She had come to see if he was alright. Said it plainly, as if those months of waiting hadn't bruised something vital inside him. She told him she had moved on, that her life had taken a different turn.

There were no details.

No reasons.

Just a statement wrapped in casual mercy.

Reginald said nothing at first. He wasn't sure how to shape words around the hollowness she had left behind. He had spent so long rehearsing what he might say if she ever came back. Questions. Accusations. Maybe even a plea. But now, standing in front of her, all of that dissolved.

He didn't ask why.

He didn't ask who.

He simply let her words sit where they landed, heavy and unwelcome.

She didn't stay long. A few minutes, perhaps. Just long enough to shatter what little hope had survived her absence. When she left, it wasn't with anger or guilt—it was with the finality of someone who had already said goodbye elsewhere.

He sat alone for a long while after she was gone. The house felt colder, though the sun had not moved. It wasn't just the loss that hurt—it was the ease with which she had handed it to him. As if what they'd shared could be folded away in a few sentences. As if he hadn't waited in winter for a version of her that no longer existed.

In that moment, Reginald felt something close inside of him. Not a door. A window, perhaps. Something smaller, but essential. A part of himself that had once believed love was enough.

He wouldn't speak of her again for years.

Not to friends. Not to the women who came after. Not even to himself, except in quiet, sleepless moments when memory slipped through the cracks. She had taken something with her—not just love, but the simplicity of believing it could not be broken.

And yet, he carried it. Carried her name in silence. Carried the weight of what was never said. Carried the lesson.

Years later, as the younger Reginald transformed into a man with suits and boots, he would come to understand that what had happened in those few short months after his final exams was not simply a failed relationship. It was a shift. A reshaping of his emotional landscape. A foundational crack in the floor of his youth that would quietly echo into his adult life. At the time, he could not have imagined that the absence of one girl, her silence, her decision, her departure, would leave such a long shadow. But it did.

In the early years after that heartbreak, Reginald found that his ability to engage with love had been altered. Something in him had broken, something vital. He had been cracked open by that first relationship, and even as the surface healed, the foundation beneath it remained changed. It was not bitterness that he carried, but distance. He dated, yes. He met other girls. He allowed himself to explore the motions of intimacy again. But somewhere deep within, he had already stopped believing that love could be what he once imagined it to be.

When those relationships ended, as they inevitably did, he didn't mourn them in the way others seemed to. There were no sleepless nights. No long letters. No lingering questions. He would simply walk away, quietly and without much reflection, as though he had long accepted that nothing real could grow in that space again. It wasn't that he had stopped feeling; it was that he had stopped investing in the possibility.

He had been shaped by that first cut. And the shape it left was cautious, guarded, and silent.

He remembers those years clearly. Not for the women he dated, but for the emotional distance he kept between himself and every possibility of love. He didn't know it then, but he had begun living in the aftermath of a heartbreak that had never been spoken aloud. That girl, his first love, had walked away, and in doing so, she had taken with her a certain innocence he would never fully recover.

And as time moved on, Reginald began to carry that silence into other areas of his life. It wasn't just relationships that became difficult—it was trust. It was vulnerability. It was the act of allowing someone else to see him in the same unguarded way. That experience had taught him, without intending to, that love was dangerous. That it could disappear without warning. That it could leave you standing alone, without answers, without explanations, and without the dignity of a proper goodbye.

There were nights, months of them, in fact, when he lived like a ghost of himself. Isolated. Numb. Moving through the world with the shell of a smile but none of its sincerity. He had sleepless nights, not from stress or ambition, but from a heart that had nowhere to go. He remembers losing weight, forgetting to eat. Not out of self-punishment, but because the appetite for life itself had dulled.

That's how deeply it hit him.

And in some quiet way, it had stayed.

Even now, as a grown man, he could still feel the faint ache of those months. He had learned to live with it, like one lives with an old injury that flares up on cold days. He had built around it. Had gone on to find love again. Had married. Had children. Had created a life that, on most days, filled him with purpose and joy. But that did not erase what came before.

The truth is, the girl from his youth left a mark that was never removed. Not because he held onto it bitterly, but because it had embedded itself so deeply into his formation that removing it would mean removing part of himself. She had become part of his emotional DNA, not by intention, but by impact. And though she no longer walked through his days, she still wandered through the corridors of his memory.

It is not something he speaks about often. In fact, it is something he kept hidden for years. Even his wife, the mother of his children, would likely struggle to hear this truth. Not because he loves her any less, but because the pain that came before her is not hers to understand. It is a separate life. A closed chapter. But one whose pages still feel warm to the touch.

If he had the chance to do things differently, he sometimes wonders, would he have held on more tightly? Would he have fought for her? Would he have tried to understand what went wrong before it was too late? Maybe. Maybe not. Because the truth is, he never really had the chance to fight. She was already gone.

What haunts him most is the silence. The not knowing. The questions that were never asked, and the answers that never came. Did she fall in love with someone else while he was away? Was there something he missed? Or was it simply the way of life—that people grow apart and don't always have the words to explain it?

That uncertainty stayed with him. It lingered in his relationships. In the way he hesitated before trusting. In the way he always seemed to have one foot out the door, just in case. It wasn't fear—it was preparation.

But life has a way of moving forward, even when your heart stays behind.

Eventually, he met the woman who would become his wife. Precious, a name that reflected her. A steady, patient, loving woman who helped him begin again. With her, he didn't just start a family, he started a new understanding of what love could be. It was not the overwhelming, all-consuming passion of youth. It was something stronger, deeper, more rooted. With her, love became less about dreaming and more about building.

And yet, even with her, he knew that a part of him had been shaped elsewhere.

He doesn't say this with regret. In fact, he says it with a strange kind of gratitude. Because that heartbreak taught him who he was when stripped of joy. It showed him the soft underbelly of his spirit, the parts of him that still hoped even when the world stopped offering promises. It introduced him to loneliness in its purest form.

And he survived it.

And that survival, more than anything, is what he carries today. It's what makes him speak gently to his children. What makes him pause before offering judgment. What makes him look at others with a little more empathy, a little more patience.

He knows now that people don't always leave because they want to. Sometimes they leave because they don't know how to stay.

And as for her—his first love—he forgave her long ago. Not through words, not through reunion, but through the resilient act of living well. Of building a life that no longer depends on the validation of her return. He hopes she is well. Wherever she is, he hopes she has found peace. Because in some way, she gave him his.

And if he could sit across from her now, not as the boy she once knew, but as the man he became, he would tell her plainly: that she hurt him, yes. But she also woke him. And in the strange arithmetic of life, both of those things matter.

This is a story he never told, not fully, not like this.

But it is part of his journey.

And if this story is to be told honestly, then the painful chapters must live beside the triumphant ones. Because the boy who was left behind at the corner of her house became the man who now stands on his own.

Chapter 6: Alone Against the World

On a Sunday morning, the man in the suit was clad in a pair of blue comfortable pajamas that he usually wore on the weekends. Precious had gone to the grocery store with his daughter, so after having a light breakfast, he went out into the garden.

He opened the garage, took out an old foldable chair, and placed it under the magnolia tree that he himself had planted when he moved here with Precious after their marriage some twenty years ago.

The sun was peeking lightly from behind the clouds, and the wind chattered as it rustled through the leaves. The man in pajamas heaved a long sigh as his eyes looked around the home he had built brick by brick, while his mind drifted away to the most dreadful time of his life

The time when he thought he had lost everything. When the only girl he had loved left him in crumbs, Rustenburg had nothing else to give him; no hope to stay back, no comfort of his grandmother, no love that it once promised. So he wiped his tears and decided to leave.

When young Reginald left the village for good, it wasn't some big decision etched out over time. There was no long goodbye. No dramatic packing of boxes. No family meeting on the porch to wish him luck. It was quiet, almost too quiet. Just a message from his uncle. A vague offer. A silent house.

His father had already gone to Johannesburg. Left a while ago. Reginald had been alone since then, walking through rooms that still smelled like old books and dried floor polish. The air inside the house had grown stale. The walls didn't echo anymore when he called out. It felt less like a home and more like a waiting room for something that never arrived.

His days had become shapeless. He'd sit outside in the winter sun, following the slow crawl of shadows across the yard. Sometimes he moved with them, shifting from one corner to the next, pretending it was a choice and not just another way to fill the silence.

There wasn't much to hold him there anymore, not after everything. The heartbreak had scorched whatever hope he had left in Rustenburg. The girl who once made Rustenburg feel like a small miracle had vanished into memory. And the people who used to ask about him had stopped asking.

So when his uncle said he had "something" for him, Reginald didn't hesitate. He didn't need details. He just needed out.

He told only one person, his cousin, the one who grew up like a brother. The one who understood the language of empty houses and full silences. The boy who knew, without explanation, that Reginald was already half gone before he even packed a bag.

They didn't have a long conversation about it. Reginald simply handed him the key to the house and said, "It's yours now. *The Doa House.* I'm going to find something. Maybe a job."

The name came from a book he had just finished reading. One of his grandmother's old Reader's Digest novels—*The Pride of the Peacock*. The main character had grand homes filled with elegant things, but he never really lived in them. Just wandered through them like a stranger. That image stuck with Reginald. He had started calling his father's house "The Doa House"—beautiful on the outside, empty on the inside.

He looked at his cousin and smiled the way people do when they're trying to make a joke land softly. "You'll be fine. You've lived in silence longer than I have."

And it was true. His cousin knew how to carry silence. His parents had always worked far from home—one with a poultry company, the other in the mines. That house had seen more ghosts than guests.

On Sunday morning, Reginald packed what little he had—just a bag with two shirts, one pair of jeans, and the only shoes he could still walk in without feeling the weight of home. He didn't write a note. He didn't leave a message. He walked out while the village still slept, his breath visible in the cold morning air.

The road ahead was not familiar. He wasn't even sure where his uncle was taking him. He only knew he wasn't coming back. Not to that version of himself. Not to that version of the village.

As he waited for the bus at the pickup point, a patch of roadside dirt worn flat by years of passengers and goodbyes, he looked back once. Not at the house, but at the idea of it. The life he thought he'd have there. The love he believed could be repaired. The version of himself that still waited for people who stopped showing up.

The air smelled of burning wood and early frost. Somewhere in the distance, a dog barked once, then fell silent.

He didn't feel fear. He didn't feel hope either. Just a kind of weightless numbness. Like his heart had finally stopped pacing, he had left the Doa House. And somewhere in that quiet, unremarkable goodbye, a new chapter had already begun.

Soon, the bus arrived with the majority of the seats empty. Perhaps more passengers will fill in along the way – people who will accompany him for a little while before he is alone again.

The bus rumbled out of Pella while the village was still asleep. Reginald sat near the window, pressed against the cold glass, watching as the dirt roads slowly gave way to stretches of tarmac and long shadows. The bus was heavy with a deafening silence. Just a few passengers, bundled in blankets and heavy coats, their heads drooping in sync with the road. He didn't speak to anyone. Just stared. Let the landscape pass like pages in a book that he no longer had the energy to read.

They reached Rustenburg around midmorning. The air there felt different, thicker, louder. A tangle of street vendors, minibus taxis, and music leaking from corner stores. Reginald had never seen so many people moving so quickly with purpose. He stood for a while near the station, holding his small bag close, trying to look like he belonged. He didn't.

Moving Up

He was supposed to get to a place called Magaliesburg, somewhere on the edges of Johannesburg, though it might as well have been on the edge of the world. He had no map. Just his uncle's instructions and a handful of change that barely got him a taxi halfway. The rest of the way, he had to hitchhike.

He remembered the hitchhiking spot someone had told him about, just outside the taxi rank where the dust hung thick and cars slowed often enough for hopeful thumbs to matter. It was the kind of place where people didn't speak much, just pointed, nodded, and climbed in. Reginald stood there for nearly an hour, shoulders aching under his bag, eyes scanning every passing vehicle. A bakkie finally stopped. The driver said nothing. He just jerked his head toward the back.

It wasn't comfortable. Cold wind hit his face and neck the entire way. But it moved him forward. And that's all he needed.

By the time he arrived, the sun was high and unforgiving. The date stuck in his memory like a stamp: Sunday, the 7th of July. He hadn't eaten since the day before. His stomach ached, but the hunger wasn't just physical. It was deeper than that. The kind that wraps around your thoughts and leaves your body too tired to argue.

The city towered around him. Roads curled and disappeared into overpasses. People walked fast, like they were late for something, even on a Sunday. On every corner, there was motion: cars weaving through intersections, people shouting across markets, children pulling at their mothers' sleeves. Somewhere in the chaos, music spilled from an open car window. A fast beat he didn't recognize.

He had never seen this kind of living. It was too much. The glass buildings. The polished storefronts. The endless flow of noise. It made the village feel like a fading photograph.

Reginald stood on the corner his uncle had described. A small shop with cracked signage and metal gates rolled halfway down. He checked the time. Then checked it again. His uncle hadn't said when he would arrive. Just told him to wait there.

So he waited.

At first, he leaned against the wall, trying to keep still. But as the hours dragged, he paced. Sat down. Stood again. His phone battery had died long before he reached the city. There was no way to call. No way to check.

By 5 PM, the sun had started to dip, casting long shadows across the pavement. The cold returned, biting and slow. He rubbed his palms together, but it didn't help much. The hunger had become sharper now, and the uncertainty louder. Was this the wrong shop? Had he misunderstood? What if his uncle wasn't coming? What if he'd just been left out here, another village boy swallowed by the city?

He thought about sleeping on the street. Where would he lie down? Would it be safe? Would anyone notice? What would his mother think if she saw him like this?

And just when the weight of those thoughts began pressing down harder than he could carry, a small car pulled up.

His uncle.

He didn't wave. Just leaned out the window and said, "Get in."

Reginald exhaled without realizing he'd been holding his breath. He climbed into the car, body stiff from standing for so long. They didn't talk much on the way back. The city lights flickered past the window like stars falling sideways.

The house was modest. A bachelor's corner; no clutter, no decoration. Just walls and furniture that served their purpose and nothing more. No smells of cooked food. No warmth was waiting in the cushions. His uncle showed him the room. A mattress in the corner. Bread on the counter. A kettle on the stove.

"Help yourself," he said, before disappearing into another room.

Reginald made tea. Spread butter on the slice of bread so thin it barely covered. Ate in silence.

That night, lying on the thin mattress under a borrowed blanket, he stared at the ceiling. His body ached in unfamiliar places, his back from the road, his feet from walking, his chest from worry. The city buzzed outside the window, even at that hour. But inside, everything was still.

It wasn't comfortable. It wasn't home. But it was something.

It was a beginning. And sometimes, that's all you need.

Young Reginald slept on a broken pillow and a worn-out mattress that reeked of stale odors. Yet, he covered his face with a clean shirt from the small that he had packed and went to sleep with his eyes tightly closed.

His first day on the job didn't come with any ceremony. He woke up and found the house empty, except for two slices of bread in a packet and a leftover egg on a plate. Reginald freshened up and swallowed the stale bread and egg with half a heart.

His uncle had left before dawn, like always. The man moved in shadows, both at work and in life. He didn't talk much about his job, just left early and came back tired. That Monday afternoon, he returned home briefly to fetch Reginald. Didn't sit down. Didn't ask how the night had been. Just said, "Let's go."

Reginald had no uniform. A pair of worn jeans, a thin hoodie, and an old pair of sneakers that barely kept the cold out. That was all he had brought from Pella, and that's what he wore on the first day.

At 4:30 PM, he was standing in line at the security company's base yard, shoulder to shoulder with men who looked like they belonged there. Men with calloused hands and deep voices. Some wore gloves. Others had thick beanies pulled down over their ears. Reginald had nothing to cover or protect himself from the cold, so he stood among them, silent, out of place, pretending he wasn't.

They called it a "parade", but there were no marching bands. Just a roll call, a briefing, and a dispatch of men into the long Johannesburg night. When they called his name, the supervisor didn't look up. Just handed him a metal baton and a location.

"You'll be on the pig farm tonight," he said. "Shift starts at six. Stay alert. Walk the perimeter. Don't start a fire. You start a fire, and you're gone."

And that was it. His training. His initiation.

By the time he got there, the last bits of sunlight were fading behind the trees. The air was sharp. The kind of cold that doesn't slap you, it creeps. Slides down the back of your neck and settles into your spine. The farm was huge. Endless rows of tin sheds. The pigs constantly made low, guttural sounds the whole night that echoed across the property. The smell hit him before he even got to the gate. Thick and sour. It curled into his nose and refused to leave.

No one welcomed him. No supervisor. No colleague. Just a chain link fence and a checkpoint station with no roof, no chair, no heater. He looked around and was welcomed by nothing but darkness. He started walking.

The baton they gave him had a small device at the end, something to register his presence at each checkpoint. Every hour, he had to pass through the same spots, tap the reader, and keep moving. No stopping. No sleeping. No shortcuts.

He hadn't eaten since morning. There had been no dinner at the house. Just the same bread, same butter, same tea. He had saved what was left, thinking he'd have it after his shift. But now, with each hour, his stomach grew louder than the pigs.

He tried not to think about it. Just kept walking back and forth. Listening to the crunch of gravel under his shoes. Watching his breath float into the night air.

There was no guardhouse to retreat to. No stove. No flask of coffee. Just him and the cold and the chorus of animals that never slept.

By midnight, his fingers were numb. He couldn't feel the baton in his hand anymore. He shoved one hand into his hoodie pocket and walked faster, trying to generate heat. It didn't help. His shoes were too thin. The cold bit straight through the soles, climbed up his legs, and settled in his chest. He didn't have gloves. He didn't have a coat. Just a body trying to stay upright.

Somewhere around 2 AM, he stopped briefly near the fence line. Just to breathe. Just to remind himself, he was still awake. The pigs grunted in the distance, restless. A light flickered from one of the barns, then went dark again.

He wanted to sit, just for a minute. But there was nowhere to sit. And he knew that if he sat, he might not get back up.

So he kept walking.

Moving Up

The checkpoints came and went. An hour at a time. Then another. Then another. The baton beeped softly in the darkness, the only proof that he was still there, still moving, still surviving.

By 5 AM, the sky had begun to lighten just slightly, a pale ribbon stretching over the horizon. He didn't feel relief. Just exhaustion. His body ached in places he didn't know could ache. His head throbbed from hunger. His lips had cracked from the cold.

He hadn't spoken a word all night. Not to anyone. Not even to himself.

When the day shift arrived, they barely looked at him. Just nodded once and took over. Reginald handed them the baton and turned away.

No one asked how the night had been. No one offered food or coffee or even a glance. It was just understood; you showed up, did your shift, and left. That was the rhythm.

Back at the house, he didn't speak to his uncle. Just slipped off his shoes, drank cold tea from the night before, and lay down on the mattress.

He didn't cry. He didn't complain. He just closed his eyes.

That first night had stripped him bare.

As his tired mind and body tried to slip into slumber, silent tears slipped from his eyes. A bittersweet memory of Pella swelled in his heart. Bitter was the love that failed him, and sweet was the love that his grandma gave him.

In the days that followed, things shifted, but not in the way that made anything easier.

Reginald finally received a full uniform. It wasn't new. The thick black coat they handed him smelled like sweat, rain, and something sour he couldn't name. It hung on a rusted hook near the outdoor bathrooms, limp and heavy, waiting for the next desperate soul to wear it. No one washed it. Everyone wore it. And somehow, the stink didn't matter when the wind cut through your clothes like broken glass. Warmth trumped dignity out there.

So Reginald put it on, zipped it up to his chin, and kept moving.

Every morning, after the night shift, the guards would pile into the back of Lady Cindy's van. She was their supervisor. Small frame, sharp voice, eyes that missed nothing. She didn't raise her weapon, but the way she spoke didn't need reinforcement. Her words stung more than any slap. She talked to them like they were replaceable. Like they had all failed something invisible, and she was just there to clean up the mess.

Reginald learned quickly not to speak unless spoken to. Not to show exhaustion. Not to ask questions.

He thought the shift would end with the sunrise. But instead of dropping them home, she took them to a nearby farm without any further explanation. They would be handed gloves with holes in them, if they were lucky, and told to gather pumpkins, some frozen solid, others already half-rotten. Their hands numbed against the frost. The smell of decay clung to their sleeves. All of it was for the pigs again. The cycle continued.

Some of the guards disappeared after the first week without any resignation letters or arguments. Just empty spots in the morning van would be there only sign of quitting.

But Reginald stayed.

Not because he wasn't tempted to leave. But because going back home and saying, *"The job was too hard"* felt heavier than the work itself. He had nothing waiting for him in the village but silence and the echo of a girl who had already moved on. He couldn't return empty-handed.

So he endured.

Two weeks in, he was posted somewhere new. A place called De Hoek Country House.

It sounded fancy, almost hopeful. But when he arrived, it was just a construction site with half-built walls and tools scattered across concrete floors. Dust hung in the air like fog. There were no finished rooms. No guard post. Just a slab of foundation, exposed pipes, and the dull clatter of men working through the day.

Moving Up

His shift wasn't a regular one. He worked through the night, and when the morning came, no one showed up to replace him. So he stayed.

Day turned into night again. Then another day. Then another night. Three full days passed, and he was still there, clad in the same uniform, the same shoes, the same body running on nothing but willpower and the dry edge of exhaustion.

There was no shower. No bed. No paycheck yet. Just a can of fish, a half loaf of bread, and a small carton of milk he had brought with him, which he rationed like treasure.

The construction workers, rough but kind, noticed him fading. They shared sips of tea. Offered leftovers from their lunches. Let him slip his feet into their blankets for a few minutes between patrols. It wasn't much, but it was enough to remind him that kindness still lived in small corners of this hard world.

He never told anyone how broken he felt during those three days.

Not the other guards. Not the contractors. Not even his uncle.

Because his uncle never asked.

He came home from his shifts, barely glanced at Reginald, and moved on with his day like nothing was unraveling in front of him. Maybe he thought Reginald would complain. Maybe he expected him to quit. But Reginald didn't. He just showed up over and over despite the cold, the silence, the missing meals, the aching limbs.

He didn't know if his uncle didn't care, or if he simply believed that suffering was the toll every man had to pay. That once you were handed a job, the rest didn't matter. That you had to earn the right to be tired. That being broken wasn't an excuse.

Reginald never asked for sympathy. But a little recognition might've gone a long way.

It was then the universe finally thought that it was enough. it sympathized with Reginald when no human in this city did. That's when he met Michael Hollenstein.

Older Reginald remembered how, after Pella broke his heart and he suffered through the nights guarding blocks and buildings, Michael had saved him and hired him as a trainee waiter at his hotel. At that time, Reginald knew only one thing: the hotel smelled better than the pig house.

He remembered how he worked his way up through hard work and loss. Until one day, at the year-end party, he was finally awarded the "Best Training Waiter of the Year."

He stood there in front of everyone, unsure whether to smile or nod. The applause was real. So was the recognition. And for a moment, he felt like he was finally becoming someone different, someone worth remembering.

But success has a strange way of reshaping your surroundings.

The others pulled back. They stopped helping him, mocking him that "the best waiters" don't need help. "You're the best," they said with mock smiles. "You should already know everything."

He didn't. Not even close.

Reginald still struggled to take proper orders. So, he found another way.

He started watching Noah, the introvert, hard-working barman from Malawi or Zambia, no one was really sure. Noah didn't talk much, but he moved with purpose. His hands were precise. His tone was respectful, no matter who stood in front of him. There was a calm about him that Reginald gravitated toward.

Little by little, Noah let him in.

He showed Reginald how to clean glassware the right way. How to pour wine without spilling. How to greet guests with warmth and clarity. Reginald began staying late, sometimes all night, just to watch, to practice, to absorb whatever he could. He didn't ask for permission. He just clocked in and didn't clock out.

Then one night, Michael noticed.

He saw Reginald behind the bar well past his hours and asked, "What are you doing here?"

Reginald froze.

Words failed him. He had no excuse that sounded professional. Just hunger and hope tangled in his throat.

Before he could answer, Noah stepped forward and said, "He's here because he wants to learn."

That was all Michael needed to hear.

The next week, Reginald was moved to the bar as a trainee.

What followed was seven years of growth, slow, quiet, and deliberate. He learned everything. Wine, coffee, service, and presence. He stood behind the bar like he belonged there. He studied menus, watched guest behavior, and practiced his smile in the mirror. He didn't just work, he became.

His first Barista Championship felt like a leap. He was one of twenty-seven. No formal training. Just instinct and preparation. He made it to the top six.

That moment lit something inside him.

Coffee wasn't just a drink anymore. It was a craft. A language. A story in a cup.

He enrolled in the Cape Wine Academy next. Paid for it himself. Weekdays with Michael, weekends wherever else would take him. On public holidays, he'd pick up extra shifts, turning down sleep in exchange for tuition.

He was never still. Never resting.

But it wasn't about proving people wrong anymore.

It was about proving himself right.

Chapter 7: Hard Labor, Heavy Heart

Proving himself right, of course, came with a cost.

From the very beginning of all this, Reginald had learned, sometimes the hard way, how to be meticulous, even when people tried to chip away at him with their careless words. Some of those remarks were tossed lightly, disguised as jokes. Others carried heavier edges, barbed with real doubt or ambition meant to mock him.

He took it all in without letting it sink too deep. Kept his head in the sky but his feet planted on the ground. Focus fixed, breath steady. He didn't always know the exact shape of his destination, but he never lost sight of where he came from. Somewhere deep inside, a quiet voice told him that if he kept moving, something good would meet him halfway.

People said whatever goes up must come down, but Reginald never lived his life calculating heights or falls. The city had already taught him that staying level-grounded, humble, was its own kind of strength. That humility was the engine that kept him pushing forward when the day felt too long and the night too cold.

There were plenty of moments when he wanted to walk away from his job entirely. In fact, he had. Three times. The first time had been nothing more than the impulsiveness of youth, a boy not yet wise to the reality that quitting wasn't just walking out the door; it came with forms, signatures, and consequences. The second time had been less foolish but no less final. By then, he'd already spent enough time living and working with the same people to know exactly how they could get under his skin. It was a love-hate arrangement, the kind that made you grit your teeth through the day and still share tea with the same people in the evening.

That second departure came during a period when he was splitting himself between work and study. For three months, he relied on his weekend "piece job" to keep the smallest trickle of income alive. It wasn't enough to live on, not really. Just enough to keep the lights on, figuratively and literally. Saturdays became a choreography of movement: college lectures in the morning, a rushed trip back in the afternoon, and then the long commute to his night shift at a job that always felt farther than it actually was.

Sundays weren't much gentler. He'd rise early, work the breakfast crowd, and then push straight through to the lunch rush. By the time the shift ended, the day's noise would still be ringing in his ears, the smells of frying oil and burnt toast clinging to his clothes.

The city was like that. It was inconsiderate and relentless. It didn't care if you were tired or if your spirit was fraying. It just kept spinning, and you either kept pace or got flung off. Reginald knew the choice he had to make, even when the work felt like it was stripping him down piece by piece.

But there was joy in that work, in the coming and fading of days that seemed, at last, to have a purpose beyond survival. When you work with people who respect your craft, the job feels lighter on your shoulders. Reginald found himself welcomed in ways he hadn't expected. The business owners liked him, not just for how he worked, but for who he was when the shift was over. They would pour him a drink, ask how his week had been, and listen without rushing him.

Victor, the man who handled his transport, became more than a colleague. Over time, he became a friend, one of the few constants in those early city years. Their bond grew quietly, in shared rides and unhurried conversations between destinations. On Saturday nights, when the streets were too dangerous for the trip home, Reginald often stayed at Victor's house. It was an unspoken arrangement. No explanations needed. By Sunday morning, he would head to work again, and when the afternoon sun began to slide down the buildings, Victor would take him back, ready to face another week.

That schedule gave him enough space to keep studying until, finally, he finished. The small certificate in his hands felt heavier than it looked, not because of the paper, but because of the road it had taken to get there.

Then came the Michael Hollenstein matter. One day, Michael asked to speak with him, but this time his tone was different. No light chatter. No polite filler. Just a direct question.

What could he do to bring Reginald back?

He said the team missed him. Reginald didn't answer right away. Life, he knew, had a strange way of circling back with opportunities, but those moments were rare.

He would later tell people he had been lucky, fortunate enough to be visited twice by what others called "the goddess of luck." His mistakes had not been born of arrogance but of not knowing better, of not having someone to show him the map. And yet, here was another chance, placed in his hands without demand or condition.

Taking it marked a shift inside him. He was no longer the young man drifting between jobs with nothing tethering him. Now there were real responsibilities that shaped his days. When his son began school, the cost of fees became his personal burden, and he carried it willingly. It was a reason to stay the course, no matter how unpredictable or sharp-edged the workplace could be.

Over time, he learned more than just the duties of the job. He began to see the architecture of opportunity, to understand the skills he would need to climb higher, to convince future employers that his work was worth not only their time but their better pay.

What he did not realize was that this struggle would drag on for seven years.

Those seven years were anything but simple. They were not, as some might dramatize, "seven years of hell," but rather a winding, uneven road that tested and shaped Reginald in ways he hadn't imagined. Some days felt like triumph. They included smooth shifts, satisfied guests, and a nod of approval from management. Other days were just survival, the clock dragging its feet while tempers flared in the kitchen or the bar filled faster than his hands could pour.

But through it all, there was growth and accumulation of skill. He learned how to manage people, how to make decisions under pressure, and how to shoulder responsibility without flinching. He even took it further, enrolling in formal management studies to give shape to what the job had been teaching him in fragments.

The bar itself became more than a counter where drinks were served; it became his window into the wider world. On quiet evenings, when the music hummed low and the glasses had all been polished, he would find himself in conversation with unexpected guests: directors of companies, leaders of NGOs, artists whose faces had been in the papers. They weren't there to teach him, but in the stillness between orders, they would drop pieces of advice like breadcrumbs. To guide him towards his destiny.

Some told him about the importance of planning beyond the paycheck. Others spoke of leadership not as control, but as the art of listening. One older gentleman, a retired diplomat, told him, "You'll go further if you learn to read people before they speak." Reginald listened closely. He was used to working without a guide, so when wisdom appeared, even in fragments, he gathered it greedily. These strangers didn't just tip in coins; they tipped in perspective.

Still, bartending had its limits. The counter could only stretch so far, and Reginald began to sense that his ambitions needed a larger room to grow in.

It was during this time that Nelson Rodriguez appeared. A man with the kind of confidence that made people lean in when he spoke. Nelson saw something in Reginald that others might have missed. Potential, yes, but also discipline, the kind of reliability that can't be faked. One afternoon, after a brief exchange, Nelson extended an invitation: come to Mount Grace, one of the most prestigious resorts in Magaliesburg.

The very thought of it stirred something in Reginald. He imagined the sprawling grounds, the polished halls, the kind of hospitality that moved beyond pouring drinks. It was an entire theatre of service. When the day of the interview arrived, he met Nelson and Kim in a glass-walled office that overlooked a manicured courtyard. Everything about the space felt intentional, from the placement of the chairs to the low hum of background music that softened the edges of the conversation.

They asked their questions with precision, not the rushed, distracted kind of queries he'd faced elsewhere. Here, each answer seemed to matter.

He remembered, almost with a wry smile, how different this felt from the ten or more interviews he had failed before. Those had been stabs in the dark. Applications for jobs in logistics, finance, and other fields far outside his reach. Sometimes he had even managed to charm his way into the room, convincing them to hear him out despite his complete lack of relevant experience. Those meetings always ended the same way: a polite rejection, sometimes softened with, "We'll keep your CV on file."

But this was different. This was his ground. By the time he walked into Mount Grace, he knew he belonged in hospitality. Not just as a bartender, but as someone who could shape experiences from the moment a guest arrived to the moment they left.

Reginald passed the interview at Mount Grace and signed a contract as a bar supervisor. It was technically a management role, though low on the hierarchy, more about keeping the bar's heartbeat steady than steering the whole ship. Still, it came with a certain pride. The name "Mount Grace" carried weight in hospitality circles, and just being part of it felt like wearing a badge of arrival.

The first weeks were filled with small victories, building rapport with the team, earning nods from regular guests, and fine-tuning service routines until they felt like second nature. Nelson would check in often, his presence steady, a reminder that someone had vouched for him, someone who saw him not just as another employee, but as a professional with a trajectory.

But then, as quietly as he had appeared, Nelson was gone. A resignation. No drama, no scandal, just a shift in the tide. Reginald felt it immediately, like a rope had been cut loose. Without Nelson, the air in the office felt different. The easy confidence he'd had in the job began to falter. He could still do the work. He did it well, but the sense of belonging that Nelson's mentorship provided had vanished.

He began looking elsewhere, scanning the landscape for another step forward. Opportunity, as it often does, came in the form of a familiar face. Nelson reached out, this time with an invitation to join him at a new establishment. There was no promise of more money; in fact, the salary was a lateral move, but the role carried heavier responsibilities. Responsibility meant growth. Growth meant more leverage for the future.

And so, he agreed.

That's how he arrived at Valley Lodge, an elegant property with an understated charm. He could picture himself there for years, shaping the guest experience, mentoring younger staff, bringing the kind of service polish that made people remember a place long after they left.

But fate has a sense of humor.

On his very first day, after a brief orientation, he learned Nelson had left the company. The news hit him like a slap, not because he couldn't work without Nelson, but because his main reason for coming had been tied to that connection. Without it, the role felt suddenly hollow. He resigned on the spot.

The management didn't rush to let him go. Instead, they insisted on verifying his appointment, which meant two weeks of waiting in a kind of limbo. He worked in the meantime, half expecting them to find a bureaucratic snag that would send him packing. But the verification came back clear. He had been properly interviewed and formally hired. With that, he officially stepped into his role.

Valley Lodge handed him not one, but two titles: floor manager and sommelier. It was a dual responsibility that required equal parts stamina and finesse. He had to oversee dining service in the day-to-day sense, while also curating and maintaining the wine program. The pace was unrelenting, but there was something satisfying about it, the way the demands pulled every ounce of skill from him and forced him to sharpen the rest.

It was during those early days that he met Lawrence McGrath. Lawrence was the kind of leader who read people quickly and thoroughly. At first, he wasn't entirely convinced of Reginald's place there. The skepticism was never hostile, but it was unmistakable. There were questions phrased just a shade sharper than necessary, a careful watching of his movements on the floor. Eventually, they sat down for a meeting. It wasn't long or drawn out, but it was enough to clear the air.

An understanding was reached. Lawrence might have doubted at first, but he also valued results, and results were what Reginald knew how to deliver.

Working with Lawrence turned out to be one of the better chapters in his career. The man was precise, demanding without being cruel, and willing to give opportunities to those who proved they could handle them. He didn't, however, raise Reginald's salary right away. "Show me," Lawrence had said plainly. "We need to grow revenue first. If you help us do that, we'll talk."

Reginald didn't flinch. He understood the bargain. In hospitality, promises were rarely signed in ink; they were earned in the math of balance sheets. So, he worked long hours, extra duties, pushing the restaurant and bar into better numbers. He trained staff, refined service sequences, and curated wine lists with an eye for both quality and margin. Slowly, the metrics turned in their favor.

True to his word, Lawrence promoted him to F&B Manager while allowing him to keep his sommelier role. It was recognition, but it also meant more hats to wear, more fires to put out, more hours on his feet. The title looked good on paper, but paper didn't pay for everything.

His son's school needs were growing. The need for uniforms, textbooks, and excursions was high, and while his salary was better than it had ever been, it still seemed to vanish too quickly. Every month felt like a balancing act between professional progress and the relentless pull of personal responsibility.

Yet, as he stood some evenings in the quiet after service, wine bottles lined neatly, the last tables cleared, he knew he was moving forward. Slowly, perhaps. At a cost, certainly. But forward, all the same.

Then came one of those rare "right moments" that slip into your life without warning, like a coin dropped into your pocket when you weren't looking.

Reginald had been without a phone for two weeks, living in that strange half-light between disconnected and free. There was a certain quietude to it. No constant buzzing, no demands leaping from the screen, but it was also a risky kind of silence in his line of work. Opportunities have a habit of calling only once.

When he finally managed to get a replacement phone, the first thing he did was check the messages. That's when he saw it. A note from Neil Martin, one of the better-known hospitality recruitment agents. The timestamp told him Neil had been trying to reach him for days. Reginald's stomach tightened. Two weeks without a reply could mean the moment had already passed.

He didn't waste another second. It was a Friday, the 11th. He called Neil immediately, his voice level but quick, letting him know the delay hadn't been neglect, just bad luck. Neil's tone on the other end was brisk but warm. "Glad you called back. I've got something for you. Sheraton Hotel in Pretoria. Interview on Monday. Beverage Manager and Assistant Restaurant Manager."

The titles hung in the air for a moment. Beverage Manager. Assistant Restaurant Manager. It was the highest role he'd ever been considered for, both in title and in pay. The kind of position that could shift the whole map of his career, and maybe even his life.

Better pay meant more breathing room for his son's school fees. It meant savings that didn't feel like wishful thinking. It meant the possibility of saying "yes" to small things without first counting every coin in his wallet.

All weekend, the idea sat with him. He didn't indulge in daydreams, not too much. He knew better than to count on a job before the ink was dry. But the thought of stepping into a role of that magnitude lit a fire inside him. He began to think through the details: his approach in the interview, the way he'd talk about his dual experience as F&B Manager and sommelier, the language of leadership and profitability that Lawrence had drilled into him at Valley Lodge.

On Sunday night, he took extra care with his suit. Pressed the jacket. Polished the shoes until they caught the light. There was something almost ceremonial about it—not just preparing clothes, but preparing a version of himself that could walk into that room and look like he belonged there.

Monday morning would come fast, and with it, a doorway he had waited years to see open.

Reginald walked into the Sheraton that Monday morning with a calm certainty that surprised even him. There was no last-minute revising of answers in the car, no silent rehearsals of phrases he thought might impress. Years of showing up, sometimes to succeed, sometimes to fail, had prepared him better than any script. The weight of past rejections had forged something steadier in him: the knowledge that he knew his craft, and that the right place would see it.

The hotel's glass doors slid open with a soft sigh, and he stepped into the polished hum of the lobby. The marble floor gleamed under the morning light, and the air was thick with the authority of a place that had seen countless arrivals and departures. He could feel the eyes of the reception staff clock him as a visitor. Their eyes moved with scrutiny, measuring his suit, his walk, the way he carried himself. In hospitality, even before you speak, you are speaking.

The interview was set in one of the hotel's side meeting rooms, where the hush of the corridors melted into the faint clinking of cups from a nearby service station. Out of twenty-one candidates, he knew most would have the technical skill for the role. The question was: who could fit the skin of it?

Nelson's earlier mentorship, Lawrence's unflinching expectations, and the wisdom of countless industry veterans had sharpened Reginald's instincts. He didn't approach this as someone hoping to impress a stranger. He walked in as though the table had been waiting for him. The questions came. He answered them without the ornamental padding of someone trying too hard, without the stutter of uncertainty. He drew on real examples, handling difficult guests, managing revenue, spotting and nurturing staff who could go further.

By the time the meeting ended, he knew. Not in the way one hopes for, but in the way a person recognizes when their voice has landed where it needed to.

Two days later, the call came. Out of twenty-one candidates, he had made the shortlist. Then, he was chosen.

Moving Up

Once again, the thread of luck, or perhaps fate, wove itself through his life.

The Sheraton was a different world altogether. Its way was sharper, its stakes higher. Every decision rippled outward, touching guests of influence, events that carried prestige, and teams that needed to be led with precision. Yet not everyone was convinced he belonged there. Some high-level colleagues eyed him with doubt, their skepticism wrapped in polite smiles. He had a sense it wasn't just about his skills—it was about where they thought someone like him should be.

One resident manager, in particular, seemed determined to push. Every morning meeting became a kind of sparring match, with questions thrown like small darts. "What's your strategy for beverage cost reduction this quarter?" "How will you address the slow turnover during weekday lunches?" The tone was clipped, the timing deliberate.

Reginald didn't flinch. He'd been through worse. He still had not forgotten cold nights on the pig farm, three-day shifts with no bed, managers who measured worth only by what they could take from you. This was different. This was a test he could pass.

Often, he was the only black person at the management table. It was a fact that carried its own weight, not because it intimidated him, but because it seemed to startle others when paired with his position and achievements. He didn't try to explain his presence; he let his work explain it.

And he worked. Hard. Not just to prove himself, but because he understood something that many forget: in the right time, effort becomes currency. Where there is will and purpose, determination steps in like a compass, pointing toward channels you didn't even know existed until you found yourself navigating them.

When he looked back on that chapter, he saw it for what it was, not just another job, but a lesson in standing your ground when the room seems to be measuring your worth against its own prejudice.

That, he thought, is my piece of hard work. And the reward was never just the position; it was knowing he had walked into the Sheraton as himself and walked out each day having stayed that way.

Looking back on his career, especially those restless, uncertain early years, older Reginald could still recall how many people had looked down on him. Some did it quietly, their doubt tucked behind polite smiles. Others made no effort to hide it. Yet, through it all, he refused to let their opinions chain him down. He worked as though no one was watching, like a dancer on a stage who needed no audience. In his own progress, he found entertainment. In his growth, he found purpose.

The world around him could be harsh. It measured people by the wrong things, where they came from, what they wore, the schools they had attended. For men like him, there were invisible ladders, and society had already decided which rung he was allowed to stand on. But Reginald would not let those invisible rules define him.

Over the years, he had learned that criticism wasn't always something to fear. Hidden inside its sting, there was often a shard of truth worth keeping. He took what was useful, discarded the rest, and used the lessons to close his own gaps. And when good things happened, he didn't boast. He stayed grounded, reminded himself that the road was long, and kept learning. Pride, he understood, was a weight he couldn't afford to carry, not when there was still so much ground left to cover.

His career had begun to take shape earlier than most would have expected. Even without the shield of formal training, he had found ways to make things work, piecing together solutions like fragments of a puzzle without a picture. He learned the modes of survival before he learned the strategies of success, leading himself before he ever led a team. That discipline of motivating, correcting, and steadying himself became the foundation of every leadership role that followed.

By the time he stepped away from management, he had spent ten years navigating its shifting tides. Ten years of choices without clear answers, of victories that buoyed him for a day and failures that stayed long enough to teach him something lasting.

Moving Up

It had never been a straight climb. Some seasons were about surviving and holding onto a position that barely held him back. Others were about leaping into the unknown, trusting that he would land somewhere worth standing. He had known hunger, both in the stomach and in the spirit, and he had known the satisfaction of walking into places where he had once been told he didn't belong.

Opportunities in those early days were rarely wrapped in silk. They came disguised as extra shifts no one wanted, added responsibilities without a raise, the casual "step in for now" that stretched into permanence. Often, the "someone better" never arrived, and he became the man for the job simply by refusing to leave.

Along the way, he met every kind of person. Mentors who handed him wisdom like a lit match, skeptics who tested him, colleagues who shared laughter after long shifts. Each one, in their own way, had shaped his journey.

There was a certain beauty, he believed, in starting with nothing. It taught the value of every resource. It made him careful with food because he had known hunger, careful with time because he had lost it before, careful with opportunities because they might never come again.

If he could speak to the boy who stepped off that bus from Pella, small bag in hand, eyes still adjusting to the city, he would tell him: *You will be underestimated. You will be overlooked. And it will hurt, but it will not break you. In fact, those will be the very things that make you.*

He would tell him that working without formal training would feel like walking into a storm without a coat, but that every storm passes. That wisdom hides in watching people, not just their words, but their movements, their choices, their treatment of those who can't offer them anything in return. That luck will come, but only to those already moving, and that readiness matters more than perfection.

He would tell him to work as though someone was watching who believed in him, even when no one did.

Leaving management hadn't been an ending so much as the folding of one page to start another. When Reginald stepped away, he carried more than a résumé. He carried a library of lessons learned in the fire. Lessons about humility, endurance, and the dignity of work done well, even in the absence of applause.

From the boy who had arrived with no plan, to the man who sat at management tables, the road had been jagged, unpredictable, and full of turns he could not have seen coming. And yet, every step had been worth it.

For in the end, it had never been just about the jobs he held. It had been about becoming the kind of man who could hold them and let them go when the time came.

That, he believed, was the true reward of hard work: not the title, not the pay, not even the recognition, but the certainty that no matter how small your beginnings or how many times you are underestimated, you can build a life that is entirely your own.

Chapter 8: Hospitality Breakthrough

There's a saying: no matter how good the dancer is, do not stay too long. Reginald understood this instinctively. Life had taught him to move before the music stopped, before the applause faded, before the crowd's attention drifted elsewhere. Staying too long in one place, especially in hospitality, could feel like standing in a room where the air was slowly running out. At first, the company noticed you, admired you, perhaps even celebrated you. But the longer you remained, the more invisible you became. Guests might return for you, yes, carrying fond memories of the way you served their wine or solved their problems, but management often stopped seeing your value. You become same as the furniture, shining and glamorous, but not noticed. Just there.

He had mastered this part of life: knowing when it was time to leave. He had lived enough years in the industry to recognize the signs—the moment when growth stopped, when every challenge felt recycled, when even victories began to taste flat. At Sheraton, he was thriving, doing some of the best work of his career, proud of the changes he had implemented, proud of the way he carried himself in rooms where few expected to see him. The hotel itself was magnificent, a structure that carried weight in the industry. But as polished as it was, Reginald sensed a restlessness inside him, the pull of something larger. He couldn't yet name it, but he knew it was waiting.

That was when Dubai appeared on the horizon.

He could recall the exact day, as if etched into his memory like a tattoo: Saturday, 31st of August, 2016. The day had begun like any other, ordinary in every detail, but by its end, his life had shifted. The interview was set for noon in Johannesburg. He arrived early, nerves tempered by the confidence that years of hard work had forged in him. But the schedule was disrupted. They moved his time to 2:00 p.m. At first, it seemed like a small inconvenience. But his Sheraton shift was set to begin at the same time in Pretoria. He was already trapped between obligations: the chance at a future he had long desired, and the present responsibilities he could not abandon.

Johannesburg to Pretoria was not a journey you could squeeze into minutes. It meant hours, traffic, and time already lost before the race even began. Still, he sat in that interview chair, the clock hammering inside his chest, and focused on the task at hand. The questions came, and he answered without hesitation. The conversation felt strangely familiar, as though he had walked into a meeting he had already prepared for long ago.

The panel didn't take long to decide. Hired on the spot. A contract slid across the table, and with it came the confirmation of his great dreams. A supervisor role, more responsibility, better pay. Reginald felt the exhilaration pulse through him. It wasn't just about the job title. It was about the recognition, the affirmation that his path, once bruised by past rejections, was finally curving toward prosperity.

What a pity that he had no time to celebrate. He rushed to work, hours late, arriving at Sheraton at 7:00 p.m. instead of the scheduled 2:00. He could have stayed away, excused himself with the reasonable justification of the interview, but Reginald had never been one to abandon responsibility. He walked in, tied himself back to his present routine, and worked until 11:00 p.m., closing the shift with the same diligence he would have given had he been there all along. A friend, the duty manager, had covered him in his absence, but Reginald finished the evening, ensuring nothing was left undone. Even when life presented him with opportunities on a silver platter, he knew discipline could not be suspended.

Sunday morning came with an urgency to make a decision. The contract from Dubai stared at him from the bedside table. Financially, it made sense. It promised the stability that his son's growing needs required. The role itself was a step forward: supervisor, a position he had once dreamed about but nearly forgotten after a failed Skype interview more than a year earlier. That memory returned to him now with irony; the application he had dismissed as lost had circled back into his life at precisely the right moment.

But it wasn't just about the money, nor the title. It was about crossing a new threshold. This job meant leaving South Africa, stepping beyond the borders he had never dared to cross. He had never even ventured to Botswana or Zimbabwe, countries so near they could be reached in a day's drive. His world until then had been circumscribed, bounded by the familiar terrain of home. Now, the new leaf of his life promised Dubai, a place he had only seen in magazines and in the stories of wealthy people

The weight of that choice pressed heavily on him. Leaving home meant leaving behind the soil that had shaped him, the streets that had hardened him, the faces that had become his compass. It meant stepping into an unknown culture, unknown rules, unknown terrain. Yet in that uncertainty, there was possibility, and Reginald had learned long ago that possibility was a currency far more valuable than comfort.

He decided to steal the opportunity.

The decision came quietly, like most life-changing moments do. He had not even freshend up after sleep when he made the decision. But that didn't mean that he did not do it consciously. He read the contract again, took out a pen from the bedside drawer, and allowed the reality to settle into his bones as he signed on the blank line next to his name. He would leave South Africa and he would walk into a world that was not yet his own. And in that leap, he would either find the man he believed himself to be, or lose him.

Looking back, older Reginald could see how precise that moment was, how delicately it balanced between past and future. Had he hesitated, had he chosen to stay in the comfort of Sheraton, his story would have been written differently. Perhaps slower, perhaps smaller. But he had chosen to move, and movement was the only constant in his life.

No matter how good the dancer is, do not stay too long.

Moving to Dubai was like stepping onto another planet. From the moment the plane landed, Reginald understood that this was no small shift in geography; it was a shift in reality itself. Higher positions always carry greater responsibility, but here, those responsibilities felt amplified, heavier, sharper at the edges. Yet with that weight came the kind of shaping that chisels a person into something new. The training alone was unlike anything he had ever experienced—intense modules on management, strategic thinking, and leadership, each designed to stretch him beyond the limits of what he thought he could endure. It wasn't just theory. It was practice, repetition, application. Each lesson demanded that he see himself differently: not just as an employee doing the work, but as someone steering, guiding, shaping.

The title of supervisor sounded smaller than what the reality demanded. On paper, the manager held the higher role, but in practice, much of the day-to-day responsibility fell squarely on Reginald's shoulders. Reporting, overseeing, guiding the staff, calming fires before they spread, holding the line when the weight threatened to bend it—those tasks became his lifestyle. At times it felt as though he was carrying more than the manager himself, but he understood that this was the nature of leadership in its rawest form. It wasn't about titles; it was about presence. And his presence was required everywhere, all the time.

One hundred and forty-four staff members reported to him daily. That number alone staggered him at first. Back in South Africa, he had managed teams before, but nothing of this magnitude. Here, every day was a roll call of diversity and discipline.

When the group of nine South Africans arrived in Dubai together, there was a kind of nervous solidarity between them. They came from different corners of the country, including Cape Town, Durban, and Johannesburg, each representing their own culture and hopes. They had all dressed formally with pressed suits and polished shoes. But the Dubai heat was merciless and suffocating. Within seconds, their formal suits were drenched and their collars stuck. That was the moment it struck Reginald fully: this was a different world. Not just another city or another hotel, but a climate, a culture, a world entirely its own. The question rose quietly in his mind: Could he survive here?

Their assignment was at Dubai Parks and Resorts, which was still under construction when they arrived. It seemed impossible at first to imagine what it could become. Concrete shells stood half-finished, scaffolding climbed across skeleton walls, and dust rose from every corner. Yet their training had already begun within those unfinished spaces. Empty rooms turned into makeshift classrooms, and from those bare beginnings, they began to prepare for something that did not yet exist. Reginald found himself amazed at how swiftly the transformation unfolded. Week by week, rubble became structure, structure became beauty. And by the time the grand opening arrived, what had once been dust and echoes had become a sprawling theme park. It was alive with color, sound, and thousands of staff from every corner of the globe.

Managing his team within that environment was both exhilarating and exhausting. Reginald was the only South African among them. His staff came from everywhere: Kenya, Uganda, Namibia, Zambia, Rwanda, Gambia, Kazakhstan, Kyrgyzstan, Ethiopia, Albania, Macedonia, Ukraine, India, Pakistan—the list felt endless. It was like the world itself had been gathered into one place, and somehow, he was expected to weave it into order. The language barriers were the first hurdle. Words that carried one meaning in English would twist into confusion when filtered through accents or cultural nuance. Sometimes he had to repeat his instructions three times, each time slower and simpler, until they landed. Misunderstandings were frequent, but so too were moments of connection. They still laughed between mispronounced words and nods of understanding when gestures filled the gaps that language could not.

Despite the challenge, Reginald found joy in the process. Training others became a source of unexpected fulfillment. He had always believed that knowledge hoarded is knowledge wasted, and here he had endless opportunities to share, to guide, to lift others. One memory stayed with him vividly: a Ukrainian colleague who significantly struggles with English. She was bright and eager, but the language barrier weighed heavily on her confidence. After hours, when most would have gone home, Reginald would sit with her and teach her. They would write words down, practice pronunciations, and work through sentences slowly until the meaning became clear. He never expected anything in return. The act itself was reward enough.

Two years passed in Dubai before he ever took an annual leave. Two years of relentless days and long nights, two years of learning, stretching and progressing. In that time, he absorbed lessons that went beyond management techniques or leadership strategies. He learned about Islam, about the UAE culture, and about the values that shaped people from every corner of the globe. He learned that hospitality was not just about food and rooms, but about understanding people, truly understanding them. Without that, service became shallow, a hollow transaction. But with it, service transformed into something richer.

When he looked back on those Dubai years, he did not see only the exhaustion or the heat or the challenges of managing a team larger than any he had imagined. He saw growth. He saw the chiseling away of fear and doubt, the sharpening of discipline, the expansion of empathy. Dubai had shown him that leadership is not about titles or the size of the team you command. It is about carrying people with you, across language, across culture, across difference, until together you create something greater than the sum of its parts.

After his two years in Dubai, Reginald felt the pull of home calling him back. The desert had taught him lessons he would carry forever: discipline, cultural sensitivity, the art of leadership across borders, but even as those lessons deepened him, they also reminded him of the soil where his journey began. He knew it was time to return to South Africa, to bring back what he had gathered abroad and let it root itself in familiar ground. His next step took him somewhere entirely new: the bush, deep in the heart of Mpumalanga.

For the first time, Reginald found himself stepping into the world of the MORE Group, where he was entrusted with managing four lodges in the Kruger National Park. It was a posting unlike any he had ever taken, and one that demanded a different kind of courage. The city had dangerous streets that could swallow you if you walked too carelessly and nights that resonated with menace, but this was nature in its rawest form. Lions, elephants, leopards, snakes, crocodiles, all of them roamed freely in the world where he was now called to serve.

His title was service manager, but the role carried far more weight than the word suggested. Here, service wasn't confined to the clink of glasses or the fold of napkins. It came with survival and respect for guests, for staff, and for the land itself. From the very beginning, he was met with tremendous support and respect. Colleagues and guests alike seemed to recognize not only the prestige of his experience abroad but the depth of knowledge he had carried back with him. Dubai had shaped him into someone larger than his own beginnings, and now that wisdom had to find its shape against the backdrop of the bush.

At first, the surroundings stunned him. The lodges were nestled in Sabi Sands, pressed close to the Sabi River, one of the most dangerous rivers in Africa. Its waters carried beauty and terror in equal measure. To stand at its edge was to be reminded of the thin line between awe and fear. He saw crocodiles with jaws that clamped down on prey like iron, pulling even strong animals beneath the current with terrifying ease. He saw lions battle rhinos, not for minutes or hours, but for days. Grueling contests of stamina and will that left the earth itself scarred where their bodies had collided. These were not glossy images on a National Geographic screen. These were scenes lived and witnessed, raw and unfiltered, pressing themselves into his memory forever.

And yet, amid all that danger, Reginald found peace. The bush tested him, stretched him, forced him to confront the deepest corners of fear, but it also grounded him. Life slowed down in a way that the city never allowed. The rhythm of nature replaced the relentless tick of the clock. He grew attuned to the cries of birds, learning their seasonal calls, their behaviors, their patterns. Each song carried meaning, each silence a warning. Slowly, he learned to read the world around him the way others read books.

Awareness became everything.

In the bush, your very survival depends on it. Awareness of every sound, every rustle, every shift in the air. A crack of a branch could signal nothing more than a bird landing, or it could mean a predator was near. Reginald learned to listen differently, to see differently, to move differently. His professional awareness sharpened alongside his personal awareness, until both became inseparable. He began to understand that awareness wasn't just a skill of survival; it was wisdom. It taught him how to read a room, how to sense a mood, how to notice what others overlooked. It was in the bush that awareness became not just a tool but a way of life.

Every six weeks or so, Reginald would return home. The journey itself was long and unyielding. Six, sometimes eight hours on the road one way, and then the same distance back. The travel was tiring, the roads often unforgiving, but it became part of his routine, an accepted toll of the life he had chosen. The moment of arrival, of seeing familiar faces and places, was worth the miles. And when it was time to leave again, he would gather himself, step back into the long road, and return to the bush with renewed determination.

At Ivory Lodge, he carried the full weight of management. The lodge demanded excellence, and Reginald delivered it, day after day. There were times when he also oversaw River Lodge, a property that carried its own story of survival. Before his arrival, it had been ravaged by fire, reduced to ruin in a matter of hours. He joined just as the rebuilding began, and he witnessed firsthand how ashes gave way to renewal. To watch River Lodge rise from devastation into beauty was more than inspiring, it was a mirror of his own journey. Out of loss, something stronger could be built. Out of destruction, something finer could emerge.

The bush was not an easy place to work, nor was it meant to be. It carried dangers both visible and hidden. Yet within those challenges, Reginald discovered a clarity he had never known in the city. The nights stretched long and dark, punctuated by the roar of lions or the call of hyenas. The mornings broke with sunlight spilling across endless horizons. Each day reminded him of the fragility and strength of life in equal measure.

Looking back, older Reginald knew that the bush taught him one of the greatest lessons of his life: the power of awareness, being observant. Not just the kind of awareness that keeps you alive when danger lurks nearby, but the kind that teaches you to truly see the world around you. To pay attention. To listen deeply. To notice what is unspoken, what is shifting, what is becoming. Awareness in the bush was survival. Awareness in life was wisdom. And in both, it was the secret that allowed him to keep moving forward.

After some time, Reginald moved again. Restlessness had always been both his curse and his compass, guiding him toward new frontiers whenever the ground beneath his feet began to feel too familiar. This time, the road carried him north, into Polokwane, a city in the Limpopo Province. It was a place that carried its own significance, not just for its geography but for its history. Polokwane was the hometown of two towering figures in South African politics—President Cyril Ramaphosa and Julius Malema. Their names carried weight across the nation, and somehow the city itself seemed to hum with the echo of their presence.

Polokwane was small compared to Johannesburg or Pretoria, but it held importance that far outweighed its size. It was home to the Peter Mokaba Stadium, a landmark etched into the national consciousness, and the headquarters of the Zion Christian Church, one of the largest and most influential religious movements in South Africa. Every year, its gatherings drew crowds so vast that the city seemed to swell beyond recognition. Reginald, arriving with the eyes of an outsider, felt that he was stepping into a place that punched far above its weight.

His work there was at the Fusion Boutique Hotel, a five-star establishment that gleamed like a jewel in the city's crown. Fusion was one of Polokwane's most prestigious hotels, catering to the elite who passed through the province for business, politics, or pilgrimage. Its polished halls and attentive service stood in stark contrast to the more rugged life of the bush where Reginald had been shaped. Here, life moved at a faster pace, and the air seemed to carry with it the constant hum of expense.

Yet, despite its charms, Polokwane never felt like home. City life had always carried a tension for Reginald. It dazzled with its lights and conveniences, but it drained with its pace and its costs. Everything seemed more expensive, more hurried, more detached from the grounding simplicity he had found in Mpumalanga. The bush had taught him awareness and peace; the city pressed him into speed and calculation. After about seven months, he knew the truth he could no longer ignore: this was not where he was meant to stay.

The decision to move on was quick and silent. One Monday afternoon, while running errands in town, his phone rang. It was one of his agents, a familiar voice carrying the possibility of change. Later that same day, he followed up on the call, and from that conversation, another doorway opened. The name attached to it was one that would soon etch itself into his career as a defining chapter: Cheetah Plains.

From the moment he set foot there, Reginald knew this was not just another lodge. Cheetah Plains was unlike anything he had encountered before. It was one of the most beautiful and high-profile properties he had ever worked at. Its reputation preceded it, whispered in hospitality circles with a mix of awe and admiration. Here, he began as Food and Beverage Manager and Sommelier, a dual responsibility that carried both the precision of service and the artistry of wine. His main charge was overseeing the wine cellars of three exclusive houses: Karula, Mvula, and Mapogo. Each house was more than a physical space; it was a story carved into the land, its name an echo of legends that still roamed the imagination of Sabi Sands.

Mapogo House bore the name of the infamous coalition of lions that once dominated the reserve. Six males, brutal in their reign, feared for their ferocity and teamwork. Their story was of power, strategy, and the ruthless balance of nature.

Karula House took its inspiration from a leopard once known in the region, a creature of grace and elusiveness, whose memory lingered in the stories told by rangers and trackers. Mvula House, by contrast, honored another leopard that was larger than most, almost lioness-sized, a creature whose presence had left an indelible mark on the reserve's history. These were not mere names chosen at random. They were monuments in their own right, tributes to the animals that had shaped the land long before any lodge was built.

Working at Cheetah Plains felt like walking in the pages of a living legend. Nights here cost upwards of ten thousand dollars, making it a destination only the ultra-wealthy could afford. The houses themselves were designed to cocoon guests in luxury, but beneath the surface lay the wild heart of Sabi Sands, always reminding even the wealthiest of visitors that they were guests in a world that belonged to something older, fiercer, untamed.

For Reginald, this chapter was about more than luxury. It was here that he polished his wine knowledge, sharpening his craft with the same meticulousness he had once applied to learning the survical in the bush. Each bottle, each pairing, each presentation became part of a larger story, one that connected culture, history, and taste. Guests from across the globe passed through those houses, and with them came conversations that widened his network and expanded his perspective.

And then, as if fate wanted to mark this chapter with something unforgettable, he found himself in front of cameras. *Top Billing*, South Africa's most iconic lifestyle television program, came to Cheetah Plains. By pure chance, Reginald featured on their very last episode before the show ended its decades-long run. There he was, on national television, presenting wines with the ease of a man who had once doubted whether he would even belong at the table. To be showcased on such a platform, and in such a place, was more than a professional highlight, it was personal vindication.

And standing in the glow of that achievement, he knew that every move, each restless departure, each leap into the unknown, had led him exactly to where he needed to be.

Chapter 9: Battles and Victories

The man in the suit, while sitting in his armchair, realized that success is never without its shadows. Even in the midst of prestige at Cheetah Plains, Reginald felt a deep yearning stir within him. In the deep thrum of his heart, he still carried the dream of working overseas. Dubai had revealed the vastness of the world, but part of him wondered what it might mean to step even further, to live beneath another sky. He had buried that desire beneath his duties, convincing himself that the bush and the wine cellars were enough. And then, unexpectedly, the world opened another door.

An American company came calling. The position was in Florida, at one of the most prestigious golf clubs near Mar-a-Lago. The offer shimmered with possibility. They offered him a salary in dollars and recognition in a land where opportunity seemed to flow endlessly. For the first time in his career, he was being valued in a currency he had only ever dreamed of holding in his own hands. Dollars. The sound of it was intoxicating.

He imagined what that life could be with palm trees swaying against the Atlantic breeze, manicured greens stretching into the horizon, a new beginning far beyond the familiar sands of Sabi. To step into America was to step into the stories he had heard since childhood, the place where dreams grew wings. It felt like vindication, proof that the long nights, the humility, the constant striving had led him to this moment. He was ready with his resignation letter already forming in his mind.

But the world is never so simple.

At Cheetah Plains, his managers—NJ and his wife, Mettie—were not prepared to let him go. They called him in and promised him a future if he stayed. They spoke of plans, of growth, of how integral he was to the story of the lodge. Their words pressed against his ambition, making him hesitate. Could he really walk away so easily? Could he abandon what had been built together, the trust, the peace, the beauty of the bush?

Reginald could not say no to his managers. However, if he had known what the future held, he would have fled to America that same day without staying even a minute longer on those bushes.

All his plans for a settled future were put on hold because of a damned virus.

COVID-19 swept across the globe like a tide that no one could stop. Borders were closed. Airports fell silent. America, so close he could almost taste it, shut its gates. The dream dissolved in an instant, replaced by the uncertainty he had never known before. The offer in Florida became something phantom, something he had once held in his hands but could no longer touch.

And yet, life did not stop. At Cheetah Plains, the pandemic brought a strange paradox. The guests were fewer, but burdens were heavier. His responsibilities multiplied while his salary shrank. He watched the figures in his paycheck fall, even as the weight on his shoulders grew. It was a bitter equation, one that tested not just his endurance but his faith in the path he had chosen.

Still, he stayed. Dumb decision, the older Reginald reprimanded.

While he was still figuring out how to maneuver his professional struggle and expenses amid COVID, tragedy struck his personal life. His younger brother, who had long been struggling with illness, passed away. For two years, tuberculosis had gnawed at his strength, leaving Reginald to carry the burden of financial support as best he could. He had sent what he could, sacrificed where he must, but family complications and poor decisions made the load heavier than it needed to be. And when his brother finally slipped away, the grief was tangled with helplessness.

COVID restrictions only added to his already piling worries. Travel across provinces was almost impossible with police checkpoints at every mile, officers blocked his way, demanding papers, doubting his truth. He was forced to pull out his brother's death certificate as proof of loss before they would let him pass. The whole journey home became an enduring humiliation doubled with sorrow.

When he finally arrived, his grief was met not with comfort but with demands. Every cent he had saved, the money he had intended for studies, perhaps even to start something of his own, was drained away. Funeral costs, cultural expectations, promises of repayment that never came: the burden of it all stripped him bare. Out of that experience, a bitter but unshakable lesson took root in him. Sometimes, family only cares when you are giving, not when you are in need.

Through it all, it was his colleagues who became his true family. They stood beside him in unity and solidarity, bridging the loneliness and grief in ways his own blood could not. Even there, cultural differences brought friction, but Reginald learned how to win people over, manage diversity, and lead with respect. In that crucible, his leadership deepened.

Yet after nearly three years at Cheetah Plains, the signs were clear. His season there was ending. The cracks had widened, the promises broken, and his restlessness for a change began to stir once again. So, he resigned and braced himself for a new horizon.

His next step carried him south to Plettenberg Bay, along the Western Cape's Garden Route, a region of breathtaking beauty, where forests dipped into oceans and vineyards sprawled across rolling hills.

But even in leaving, he could not escape without scars. Cheetah Plains withheld his final salary and overtime, something so low that he did not expect it. It was a betrayal that stung deeply. He even pursued a legal case, but the owners were too wealthy, too protected, for justice to find its way. The stress bore down on him until his body itself rebelled. Hypertension gripped him. There were moments when he collapsed, feeling life itself slipping away under the sheer weight of it all.

And yet, he endured. Once again.

In Plettenberg, he rebuilt himself piece by piece. He became General Restaurant Manager, leading a brilliant team with the authority of experience and the humility of hardship. Slowly, he made a name for himself in the heart of the wine lands. He met winemakers from every corner of the region, shared stories and ideas, and reawakened the part of himself that found joy in flavor, craft, and community. For a while, he allowed himself to forget his troubles, to breathe again, and to taste life as it was meant to be lived.

***

There were words that lingered with Reginald, even years later, words he had once heard from Nelson Mandela. The phrasing had blurred in his memory, but the essence remained sharp. Mandela had spoken of men and women across the world, how some left no mark at all, while others left scars with their malicious deeds. At some point, Mandela had turned to forgiveness, explaining that forgiving did not mean condoning misbehavior or trusting those who had wronged you. Forgiveness, he said, was for the self, for the freedom to live one's own life unchained by bitterness.

Those words planted themselves deep in Reginald's heart, but they did not grow there alone. Forgiveness had been sown in him long before, by his grandmother's sweet voice. She had taught him to let go, to move on, to resist the temptation of dwelling too long on harm done. "That's how life is," she would say. And Reginald had come to believe it: that forgiveness was not weakness but wisdom, a survival tool, a way of keeping one's spirit intact when the world seemed intent on bruising it.

For his background—school, work, and everything in between—had carried the weight of disgrace. He had been named, labeled, dismissed in ways both subtle and harsh. And what struck him most was that it was never just about one color or one culture. The labels seemed to cross every line, coming from all directions. Perhaps, he thought, it was because people felt threatened. Change unsettled those who had already grown comfortable, and he brought change into every space he entered, whether through education, through discipline, or through sheer presence.

Workplaces, he learned, had their own culture of resistance. It was not always open hostility. Often it came cloaked in politeness, in silence, in small acts of exclusion. He would not simply call it jealousy, though jealousy lurked in its shadows. No, it was something subtler, more corrosive: the refusal to support, the refusal to embrace what was good simply because it came from someone unexpected. He learned this the hard way. Time after time, he found that the fiercest challenges did not always come from competitors outside the building, but from colleagues beside him, or from those above him, unwilling to see him rise.

These experiences tore him apart more than once. They broke his heart, scratched away his belief in fairness. At times, the only way to protect himself was to leave, not in anger, not in open rebellion, but in raising a white flag of peace and retreat. He believed in peace, even when peace meant walking away. Fighting back, for him, did not mean shouting or clashing. It meant taking time to reflect, to rebuild, to move forward in spite of being disgraced for trying—for daring to learn, for daring to show skill in front of colleagues who should have celebrated his growth.

It had been a challenge in every company he worked for, from his earliest days to the heights of his career. The sting of it never left him. He could still recall the first time it happened, when he was still young and just beginning to imagine a future. He had overheard colleagues laughing behind his back:

"How does he think going to school will help him? Just for a small certificate?"

"How does he think he'll end up owning an office? He's just dreaming."

Those words cut deep, sharper than any physical wound. They settled like a knife between his shoulders, carried with him long after the voices faded. Words like that created a distance, a separation between him and those around him. Yes, he could celebrate with colleagues, but he always celebrated with caution, knowing who stood beside him and what they might secretly think.

There was an old saying he held close: keep your enemies near, so you know their plans. Reginald believed in it. Sometimes, he trusted strangers more than so-called friends. A stranger might calculate your moves, but at least you expected it. A close friend's betrayal, on the other hand, could tear far deeper. That was a truth he had lived, and one he never forgot.

**

It was true, Reginald often thought: iron sharpens iron. Work had been that sharpening force in his life. Every company he had entered carried its own set of

114

insults, challenges, and pressures designed, whether intentionally or not, to break him, to make him quit. Yet he never retaliated. He placed those struggles into God's hands.

Reginald was not the kind of man one would see in church every Sunday, but he prayed every single day. Prayer was his lifeline. In his quiet moments, he prayed even for those who had wronged him, not that they might suffer as he had, but that they might prosper, that life would open itself to them in better ways. It was his way of digesting pain, of transforming bitterness into something that did not poison him. Forgiveness was not passive for him; it was active, a discipline rooted in faith and practiced in hope.

People judged quickly, often without understanding how elastic the human mind could be, how much a person could achieve when stretched by hardship. Reginald's resilience had not been built in the polished halls of hotels or luxury lodges. It had been forged in the simplicity and difficulty of his upbringing. He remembered waking before dawn to prepare firewood, boiling water just to bathe, cooking meals the slow, laborious way. Those lessons of survival included patience, courage, and a refusal to shy away from difficulties. They were the silent teachers of his life, lessons carried into every workplace and every challenge.

In South Africa, culture itself revealed its contradictions. He had seen people wear their best suits on Sunday mornings, carrying Bibles with solemn faces, only to find them the next day in pubs, their lives echoing the opposite of their proclamations. Such moments reminded him that appearances could not be trusted, that life required discernment, and that human beings were often far more complicated than their public masks suggested.

Books, too, had shaped him, sometimes more deeply than people. Among them, one stood out: *The Art of War* by Sun Tzu. The strategies in those pages became more than theory; they became armor for the workplace. They showed him how to withstand insults, how to face ridicule, how to manage when others sought to undermine him. Again and again, he found himself handed heavier tasks than his peers, deliberate attempts to see him falter. But he carried those weights with endurance, drawing on the discipline of his past and the strategy of his studies.

When the burden grew too heavy, when resentment threatened to take root, he chose to leave rather than allow bitterness to define him. For Reginald, leaving was not a failure. It was preservation of dignity, of memory, of peace. He wanted each chapter to close with good memories, not fractured ones. Wherever he went, he hoped to be remembered not for the battles he endured, but for the grace with which he endured them.

One lesson that stayed with Reginald came from an unexpected source: Bernard Botha, a brewer in Magaliesburg. During his studies in business management, Reginald had been assigned an entrepreneurship project that required him to interview a business owner. It was a cold winter Sunday when he found himself seated with Bernard, the scent of hops and malt drifting through the air as the man shared his philosophy.

Bernard kept his advice simple. Three principles that had shaped his own pat

1. Respect your family.
2. Always enjoy your life.
3. No matter what, be humble.

He leaned back after listing them, his tone carrying the kind of weight that comes only from lived experience. "Attitude," Bernard told him, "not knowledge, not wealth—that's what takes you far."

Those words struck something deep in Reginald. He had spent so much of his life chasing knowledge, building skill, proving himself worthy in spaces that doubted him. Yet here was a reminder that beyond certificates and accolades, it was attitude that carried the greatest power—the way one carried oneself in hardship, the way one treated others, the humility that steadied a man even when the world tried to shake him.

He carried Bernard's wisdom with him into every step of his life that followed. Respect, joy, and humility became anchors, reminders that even as ambition pulled him forward, it was his attitude that would determine how far and how honorably he could go.

The greatest of his life lessons were taught, not by failure and hardships, but by his grandmother, at an age when his mind was too little to fathom them.

Reginald often thought of his grandmother and the lessons she fed him along with little morsels of food, especially when life pressed in on him the hardest. She had lived with only one hand, a disability that drew stares and cruel words from others, yet she carried herself with unshakable dignity. Where others might have wilted under mockery, she walked with love, respect, and humility. Her example was a promising sermon he carried throughout his life: that a person's worth was never determined by what others saw missing, but by how one held themselves in the face of insult. From her, he learned to carry wounds without allowing them to become chains.

But forgiveness, this gift she had planted in him, was never easy. Reginald understood this truth deeply. Many people, he realized, did not even know how to forgive themselves, let alone extend forgiveness to others. Yet forgiveness, when practiced, was liberating. It lightened the spirit, freed the body from the toxins of resentment. He often thought of the story of the students who were asked to carry bags of tomatoes, each tomato representing a grudge. At first, the bags seemed bearable, but soon the tomatoes rotted, stinking and weighing the students down. Holding grudges, he realized, was no different. If carried too long, they poisoned the one who held them.

He had learned this lesson the hard way. There was a time when stress had overwhelmed him so completely that he collapsed. Doctors warned him then that stress was not a passing discomfort but a force that could end his life if left unchecked. From that day forward, Reginald made a vow: he would not allow pain to fester inside him. He would forgive. He would move on. He would smile, even when his heart was breaking. That smile became his shield, his medicine, and sometimes his rebellion. It healed him, softened anger, and turned battles into victories no one else could see.

Even when those who had once hurt him later returned asking for help, he did not turn them away. He gave what he could, offered support when needed. Life's wheel, he believed, always turned back around. To respond with generosity, even when bitterness would have been easier, was part of what made him whole.

Workplaces had sharpened that lesson. He had long stopped calling colleagues "friends." Experience taught him that friendships at work could be more dangerous than open rivalry. Strangers, at least, revealed their intentions. Friends could wound more deeply because they were trusted. And so, when environments grew toxic, Reginald chose to walk away, to be alone, to be at peace. In isolation, he found space to think, to learn, to grow. It made him fearless, because he knew exactly where he stood with himself, and that was enough.

Yes, he had carried much in his life. Insults, betrayals, losses. But what defined him was not the pain, but the way he chose to respond: through forgiveness, through forgetting, through carrying scars as lessons and wearing humility as his armor. Above all, he carried a smile. That was who he was.

After all the life and love experiences he had endured and faced in solitude, Reginald could look back and see a transformation. He had walked through flames, and though the fire had burned, it had also forged. At times, he wondered what his life might have been had it been smoother, easier. Would he have been gentler? Softer? Less restless? Perhaps. But he also knew that without those raging trials, he would never have become the strongest version of himself.

Still, questions haunted him, especially when he thought of his childhood. Would life have been different if he had grown up with both parents by his side? What if his father had stayed? What if his mother and father had been able to show him, together, the love he so often craved? These questions came like echoes he could never silence. And yet, he learned to accept that answers would never come. His parents themselves had never explained what went wrong between them, never laid bare the choices that had splintered his childhood. Some mysteries, he realized, one must carry without solution.

The real strength, he discovered, was not in seeking answers but in turning wounds into wisdom. Negative moments could be reshaped, if one chose to see them differently. Not everyone had that ability, but Reginald lived by it. He had walked through grief, betrayal, and loss, and yet he emerged each time with something greater than before. He had buried friends and family, and though grief clawed at him, he refused to drown in sorrow. He had taught himself not to break, but to bend, and in bending, to grow.

This resilience gave him independence. He seldom sought advice from others. Outside voices, he had learned, could often confuse more than clarify. Instead, he became his own guide. He spoke to himself, reasoned through choices, and trusted his instincts. Especially in his darkest moments, it was this inner compass that kept him moving forward.

Failures and setbacks never registered as final blows. To him, they were simply new challenges, another side of the coin of life. Each difficulty lit a new fire in him, awakening hunger to understand more, to believe in better days ahead. Pain, for him, was not the end but the beginning of new strength. He worked hard to turn negativity into fuel, into pathways forward that others might have missed.

Looking back on his career, Reginald remembered the voices of those who had doubted him in the early days. They had laughed, dismissed his education, mocked his ambitions. But he did not let their judgment define him. Instead, he moved like a dancer on a stage, performing as if no one was watching, delighting in his own growth and progress. He entertained himself with how far he could go, even when others refused to see it.

Society could be harsh, he knew. It labeled, judged, whispered. But he had chosen never to let those voices hold the pen to his story. Criticism, he learned, could be a teacher. Even the cruelest words carried fragments of truth if one was willing to extract them. He took what could help him grow and discarded the rest. And when success came, he wore it lightly. He did not boast, did not parade his victories. He stayed grounded, kept learning, kept sharpening himself like iron against iron.

His career, in hindsight, had blossomed quickly. Even without formal training in the beginning, he found ways to figure things out, to survive, to lead himself long before he led others. By the time he entered management, he had already spent years navigating storms of rejection, moments of triumph, and seasons of hardship. He carried them all, not as burdens but as badges.

It had been a wild ride. Ten years of highs and lows, of being underestimated and then proving himself, of joy and sorrow, of beginnings and endings. Through it all, he embraced the whole journey. For Reginald, life was not meant to be lived free of hardship. It was meant to be lived fully, with hardship included, each scar a line in the story of becoming. And through forgiveness, humility, and endurance, he had become a man even stronger than the boy inside him had ever imagined.

He had grown in unbelievable ways. From dumb decisions to planned strategies, he had come a long way ahead. Reginald could still remember the first overseas offer he ever received in Ajman, in the United Arab Emirates. It was an opportunity many in his field would have seized without hesitation, but he turned it down. At the time, he didn't understand foreign currency. He looked at the numbers, compared them to what he earned in South Africa, and dismissed the offer as too small. Only later did he realize his mistake. The salary was worth four or five times what he had been earning. Ignorance had cost him his first chance at leaving the country.

He carried that disappointment like a private reminder until he chose to educate himself. He studied currencies, learned the value of what the world was offering beyond his borders, and prepared himself for the next chance. It took a year of patience and persistence, but eventually another offer came. This time, he was ready. He didn't even have a passport then, but he found a way, made it happen, and boarded a plane for the first time in his life.

The memory of that flight, of stepping into the unknown with courage, never left him. That was when he finally understood what people meant when they said, *"The sky is the limit."* For him, it was not a cliché. It was the truth written across the clouds he soared through.

In that moment, his thoughts turned to his grandmother. How he wished she had lived to see that version of him, the man who had risen from humble beginnings to cross oceans. He owed her everything: her blessings, her teachings, her gentle insistence on humility and forgiveness. She had given him the tools he needed to survive a world that often mocked and misunderstood him. She had believed in him without ever seeing the heights he would reach.

From his father's side, there had been grandparents as well. They had made promises of support but never followed through. Yet Reginald chose not to harbor bitterness. In the end, he believed, parents bore the responsibility, and after a certain age, he understood that no one else would carry his burdens. He was on his own. And from that point forward, he embraced that truth.

Reginald had walked his journey largely alone. He was definitely scarred but unbroken, tested but unyielding. And in carrying himself with forgiveness, humility, and determination, he had proven that even the harshest beginnings could grow into something extraordinary. His story, he knew, was not just about survival. It was about becoming. And he became what his grandmother always taught him to be.

Chapter 10: All and Everything at once

It was when Reginald was still working at the Cheetah Plains, and when COVID-19 struck the world, that he realized how utterly insignificant yet significant his life was. Viewed from the vastness of the universe, his life and body were just a speck that made a negligible difference, but to his family, he was the whole universe.

In 2021, he contracted the virus, and then Reginald's life changed in ways he could never have imagined. Until then, he had considered himself resilient, almost immune to the invisible blows of fate. But the virus arrived like a thief in the night. It made him doubt his certainty and resolve. For him, it was not just the world that shut down—it was also his own body that was affected.

Hypertension, a condition he had never imagined would follow him. His days at Cheetah Plains had taught him endurance; his struggles with managers and withheld salaries had taught him patience. But this new battle was different. It was not with people, nor with institutions, but with his own body, which was becoming fragile with each passing day.

He remembered vividly when the Delta variant seized him. It was symptomatic of pushing through the discomfort of fatigue at work, and the next thing he knew, he was locked inside a room at Cheetah Plains, isolated, fighting for breath. On the sixth day, when the air seemed to vanish from his lungs, he lay in bed certain that it was his last night alive. The silence of that room felt like a coffin. He tried to pray, but even his whispers broke into wheezes. In the middle of the night, chest heaving, he thought of his children, of the life not yet lived, of the wine he had not yet poured, the stories he had not yet told. And he thought: *So this is how it ends.*

But morning came. Somehow, against the tide of fever and suffocation, he survived. And yet, the pain of the night left its mark. For the next month or so, he was quarantined inside his small room. No one was allowed to meet him, nor was he allowed to step outside. Those moments of exile made him miss every aspect of his mundane life, most of all, his family. He connected to them through FaceTime, and their pixelated faces and buffered voices made him even more upset. He missed them direly, yet couldn't meet them.

Even long after recovery, a dull ache persisted beneath his heart, an invisible reminder that life could vanish in an instant. Doctors ran tests and told him he was healthy. But Reginald knew what he felt. The pain came and went like an uninvited guest, and with it, a constant reminder of mortality.

It was during those four weeks of solitude that something different shifted within him. He found books—whatever was at hand, scattered magazines, dog-eared paperbacks left by guests, even training manuals. Anything with words became a lifeline. Reading filled the emptiness of the room, shaping his mind, redirecting his thoughts. He found himself drawn to philosophy, to leadership, to the stories of men and women who had endured storms of their own. Slowly, he realized that survival was not just physical. It was also spiritual, mental, and emotional.

When he walked out of isolation, he was not only physically better, but also mentally. He knew he could no longer live on half-dreams and deferred ambitions. The near-death experience had stripped him raw, and in that rawness, he uncovered the truth about life. COVID had stolen much, but it had also given him resolve.

That resolve soon found structure in an unexpected form: *MyGrow.* The program seemed almost too simple initially. Daily exercises. Reflections. Questions that felt easy to dismiss: *What good thing did you do today? How did it impact others?* But as days turned into weeks, Reginald realized that these were not small tasks at all. They were chisels, slowly carving away the doubt, fear, and hesitation that had lingered within him.

When he was asked to serve as a team leader of his group for a project, he almost laughed. Leadership in the bush, in restaurants, in the chaos of hospitality—those he knew. But leading colleagues in reflection? Guiding managers through vulnerability? That was new. Yet he rose to it. He learned to listen more deeply, to hold people accountable not by force but by encouragement. He discovered that leadership was not always about giving orders. Sometimes, it was about reminding people of their own strength.

MyGrow became more than a course. Like a mirror, it showed him his flaws, but also his capacity to grow. It rekindled his self-confidence and gave him new tools for resilience. In many ways, it was a continuation of what the virus had begun: the reshaping of his inner life.

At work, his renewed sense of self was noticed. Managers appreciated him, not just for his efficiency but for the dignity and charm with which he carried himself. For years, he had felt invisible, fighting for acknowledgment. Now, recognition came naturally. In the middle of uncertainty, he felt valued. That, he realized, was its own kind of wealth.

And yet, even as work affirmed him, his heart carried an emptiness. He was far from family, from the laughter of his children, from the warmth of kinship.

After COVID, and after his job in Plettenberg, Reginald has started to live and work on a cruise where he is the Sommelier and works with wine

The cruise ship has become both refuge and exile.

Life onboard is a world of its own. Cabins are no larger than closets, shared with men from different nations, each carrying their own tempers, habits, and silences. He has learned quickly that survival here is not about physical strength but about emotional balance. To live on a ship is to live in constant negotiation—with space, with personalities, with solitude.

Some nights, Reginald lies in his narrow bed listening to the groan of the sea against the hull and thinks of home. The ship is a marvel, but it is also a confinement. He has to protect his peace, guard his thoughts, and remind himself daily to smile. That smile, once a shield in the workplace, has become his compass on the waves.

Patience is his anchor. Awareness is his tool. He has learned which conversations to enter and which to avoid, when to extend kindness and when to guard his energy.

On land, one can walk away from conflict. At sea, there is no escape. Harmony must be built, or at least maintained, for the sake of survival.

Still, there are moments of beauty. Sunsets paint the sky in colors he has never seen. The sea reminds him that life is vast, unpredictable, and constantly in motion. In those moments, he feels small but also strangely free.

And yet, when he closes his eyes, it is not the ocean that fills his heart. It is his family. The thought of his children growing, changing, building lives in his absence has been both his strength and his sorrow. He values them more than words can hold. Every sacrifice he makes on the ship, every long shift, every smile he forces, is for them.

He misses the simplicity of being near them: the sound of voices echoing in a house, the rhythm of ordinary days, the laughter around a shared meal. Out here, he has prestige, recognition, and opportunity. But what he longs for most are the small, unremarkable moments that can never be replaced.

Reginald knows he is alive by grace. He has survived storms of illness, injustice, and grief. He has rebuilt himself again and again. But through it all, one truth has become clearer than any other: life is too short not to treasure the people you love. Even as he sails across oceans, as he pours wine for strangers and smiles through the loneliness, his heart is anchored at home.

It is his family that he missed, valued, and cherished, the one thing that gives meaning to everything else.

Part 2:

The man on the cruise is well aware of the importance of his family. Just as much as he struggled with his career and growth, he could not thank God enough for the family he was blessed with at a really early stage of life. It was as if he was climbing two stairs at a time. The balancing factor between the two stairs? Precious. His wife. The sturdy railing between his children and career.

Reginald was still in his early twenties when life handed him its heaviest crown. He had met Precious not long before, and already the world was rearranging itself around them. It had not been a long courtship filled with luxury or time for games. He had been working since his teenage years, already carrying responsibilities that left little space for childish experiments. But the moment the news came that they were expecting a child, something deep inside him shifted. It was not fear alone. However, fear was there, sharp and undeniable. It was the knowledge that childhood itself had ended. He was stepping into fatherhood, a place where nothing could be taken lightly.

At first, the thought of being a father at such a young age felt almost surreal. He tried to imagine what it would mean, how his daily life would change. And then the reality struck him: fatherhood was not an idea; it was a demand. It meant rearranging his whole mindset, learning to carry burdens without complaint, and learning to save every cent because there was no room for waste anymore. He could not afford to live as he once did, spending loosely on fleeting pleasures. There was now someone else whose life depended on him.

He often thought of it as standing at a crossroads, the past on one side, the future on the other. In the past, he was a young man, earning his first money, spending it as he pleased. In the future, he was a father, a provider, a man bound by responsibility. The choice had already been made for him the moment Precious carried their child within her. There was no turning back. He knew he wanted to give that child everything he himself had never received—love, care, stability, protection. And with that decision came a fire inside him, a determination to become what his own life had denied him.

Moving Up

Precious walked beside him through those early days, and together they faced the weight of expectation. Parenthood did not come with a manual. There were no elders constantly whispering instructions in their ears. They had to learn as they went, fumbling in the dark, making mistakes, yet trying always to shield their child from the worst of their inexperience.

Reginald sometimes sat awake at night, staring at the ceiling and thinking of what kind of father he could be. His own childhood had been full of gaps, absences, and unanswered questions. He vowed that his children would never know the gnawing hunger he once felt, the shame of lacking food or clothes, the loneliness of a house without love. Even if all he had was little, he would stretch it to cover every need.

When his son, Onkarabile, finally came, life changed overnight. Suddenly, sleep was a luxury. Fatherhood was a twenty-four-hour job, relentless and unyielding. Between his work, his studies, and the cries of a newborn, Reginald felt the world pressing down on him from every side. But the surprising thing was this: the exhaustion did not crush him. It refined him. Each sleepless night taught him patience. Each diaper, each bottle, each late-night worry only made him more resilient.

He learned that commitment was not about grand gestures; it was about showing up, again and again, even when the body begged to stop. He carried his responsibilities like bricks on his back, sometimes trembling under the load, but never setting them down. Precious was his partner in this struggle, and he marveled at her strength. If he was the provider, she was the nurturer, the constant presence that made their small family feel like home.

There were moments when Reginald wondered if the world was testing him too soon. Other men his age were still chasing freedom, drifting through parties, unbound by responsibility. But for him, every morning began with the same thought: *I have someone depending on me.* That awareness gave him a reason to wake up, to endure long hours at work, to sacrifice his desires. It was not motivation, he realized—it was necessity. A necessity shaped by love.

He thought often of his son's future. He wanted him to walk into a brighter life, free from the struggles that had shaped his own boyhood. He wanted his children to rewrite the story of their lineage, to live without carrying the ancestral burdens that had weighed him down. "They are not here to relive my life," he often said to himself. "I have lived my journey. They must live theirs."

Yet fatherhood also came with distance. Work took him away, sometimes for weeks, and in those absences, Precious became the anchor of their household. Reginald admired her strength but also felt the sting of guilt. He knew that his role as provider often left her alone to shoulder what should have been shared. Still, he reminded himself that one day, when the children were grown, they would see the meaning behind his sacrifices. They would know that his absence was not abandonment but love, expressed in the only way he could afford at the time—through provision, through the silent gift of stability.

Technology became his bridge across the miles. Where once a father would have been cut off, forced to live with the ache of separation, Reginald had phones and video calls. He clung to those conversations, even when teenagers on the other side of the line gave only brief, reluctant answers. It was not the same as presence, but it was something. And sometimes, something was enough to keep the bond alive.

Still, worry gnawed at him. Was he giving enough love? Was his absence scarring them in ways they could not yet express? These thoughts kept him humble, forcing him to check himself, to make sure that whenever he was home, he poured love into the gaps his work had created.

When he was free and all by himself, he thought about Precious. She was not just his wife but the unseen pillar of their family, the one who transformed his financial support into a life of order and nurture for the children. Without her, he often admitted, everything would have fallen apart. She was the one who turned sacrifice into survival, who bore the silent stress of carrying his burdens alongside her own. To him, she was not just Precious by name, but by nature.

Reginald often remembered the libraries he visited during those days, places where he spent hours studying amidst fatherhood and work. He would escape the noise of home, sit among the rows of books, and try to feed his mind while his heart worried about the family waiting for him. He knew that every hour he spent there was an hour stolen from them, yet he believed the knowledge would one day bring them a better life. It was a difficult balance, and guilt was never far away, but he endured it with the hope that his sacrifice would blossom into reward.

The journey was not without tension. Sometimes he collapsed under stress, sometimes guilt gnawed at him. But then he looked at his son—growing, thriving, turning into a man—and he felt pride swell in his chest. Whatever he had done wrong, he knew he had done one thing right: he had given his children the foundation he himself never had.

Fatherhood, he came to understand, was not a task that ended when the children grew older. It was lifelong. It was being available, in spirit if not always in body, guiding them through the storms of adolescence, offering advice when asked and prayers when not. It was preparing, even now, for the day he would be a grandfather, ready to fill the gaps he once left, ready to turn regret into redemption.

Looking back, Reginald could see clearly how far he had come from the young man who once lived for himself. Fatherhood had reshaped him, refined him, hardened him and softened him all at once. It had been his greatest burden, and yet also his greatest blessing.

And through it all, Precious remained by his side. Together, they built not just a family, but a legacy. A legacy of love, resilience, and hope—one that would ripple forward into generations yet unborn.

Reginald often told himself that fatherhood was not about choice but about reason. There was always a reason to rise in the morning, to put on his shoes, to face the grind of another long day. It was not a game. It was not for applause. It was because someone out there depended on him. His children were not ornaments to be admired from afar—they were his responsibility, the reason his back carried burdens heavier than most men his age had ever imagined.

As the years moved forward, he discovered that raising children was not a straight path. With every stage of growth came new challenges, and with every challenge came the need for new strength. He admitted to himself often that he had no manual, no perfect blueprint for how to raise a child. He and Precious learned as they went along, fumbling sometimes, but always trying to shield their son from the cracks in their learning. It was only God's strength, he believed, that carried them through the ups and downs, the long nights and the uncertain mornings.

The years etched their stories quietly. Reginald could look at his son now, eighteen years old, no longer a boy but a young man stepping into his own. He felt both astonishment and pride. When the boy looked at him, Reginald thought he saw more than just a father; he saw a man who had endured storms for his sake. It was a pride shared, though, between him and Precious. Together, they had built this foundation, not perfectly, but faithfully.

What struck Reginald most was the way his son had grown up watching. The boy had seen his struggles, his sacrifices, his constant departures and returns. He had seen him leave for work, sometimes with only a few words of explanation, and he had seen him return with arms weary but open. That silent observation had been its own form of education. Reginald had spoken to him, yes, shared lessons about life and resilience, but the boy had also learned simply by watching. Children, Reginald realized, often understood more than they let on.

The children did not always understand, especially when they were young. But as the years passed, they began to accept the reality of it. They knew that absence was not neglect, that love was not measured only by presence. And when he returned, the family celebrated the moments together. Laughter came easily in those reunions, because they all knew that life was too short to waste on silence or resentment.

Reginald often thought of how different things might have been twenty or thirty years earlier, before technology built its bridges. If he had been a father in those days, away from home, he would have been a ghost, cut off by distance. But with phones, video calls, and messages sent across oceans in seconds, he found ways to remain present even in absence. Technology did not erase the longing, but it made the burden bearable.

He carried this duality within him—the pride of being a provider and the guilt of being away. At times, it pressed heavily on him, especially when Precious carried the household alone. He knew she bore the weight of his absence as much as she celebrated his presence. He had come to see her not only as his wife but as the invisible hero of their family story. Without her patience, her endurance, her relentless love for the children, everything would have collapsed.

Sometimes, late at night, he wondered if his children truly understood what he had endured for them. Perhaps they did not yet. Perhaps they would only come to understand when they became parents themselves. For now, it was enough that they had food, clothing, education, and love. Things he had once thought of as luxuries but which he fought to make their birthright.

He was determined to pass on not bitterness but hope. The next generation, he believed, could rise above the scars of the past. If he had carried pain, let it end with him. His children would not relive it. They would create something new, something better. That was the vow he renewed each day, with every step into the grind of work, with every mile of separation from home.

Fatherhood had taught him that life was not about waiting for choices; it was about shouldering reasons. Reasons to work, reasons to sacrifice, reasons to endure. His children were those reasons. They were the anchor that steadied him in storms, the fire that pushed him through exhaustion, the legacy he wanted to leave behind.

And as he thought of the future, of his son turning eighteen and stepping into manhood, Reginald felt both fear and hope. Fear, because the world was ruthless, unpredictable, filled with the same struggles that had once broken him. Hope, because he believed his son was better prepared than he had ever been. With

Precious's love and his own lessons woven into him, the boy had everything he needed to write a story brighter than his father's.

For Reginald, that was enough. That was the victory hidden inside all the years of sacrifice.

What gave him the most pride was not material. It was knowing that his children felt loved by their mother, by him, even when oceans separated them. Physically, he might have been away, but emotionally and spiritually, he was always present. That was the love he had lacked in his own childhood, the absence he swore he would never pass on.

He and Precious had chosen to create their own way of life, apart from the weight of ancestral behaviors and generational shadows. They wanted their children to know guidance, not chains; freedom, not inherited wounds. What had happened thirty years earlier in his own story did not need to be retold in theirs. For them, it would be a fairy tale, a lesson in history, but not a destiny.

When he looked at his family, Reginald saw a bright horizon. He felt pride in the work they had done, in the way the children had been brought up, in the unity that bound them. But he could never tell the story without naming Precious. She was the constant, the one who had made their dream of family into a reality. He was a father, yes, but she was the heart of their household. Every success belonged as much to her as to him.

Together, they had endured hurdles, endured separation, endured storms. And still they stood, moving forward together. Reginald often said it was the most precious gift of his life. That, after everything, they were still one solid family. Precious by name, Precious by nature, she embodied the treasure of his journey.

When he looked down memory lane, he did not see perfection, but he saw resilience. He saw love that had endured, a bond that had held firm, children growing into their own, and a marriage still rooted in companionship and faith. It was, to him, the one love of a single, solid family.

Chapter 11: The Kit Cats

Life has a way of breaking expectations. Sometimes it breaks them in painful ways, and sometimes in ways that open doors to joys they never imagined. For Reginald, fatherhood carried both blessings and sorrows, each child teaching him lessons that no workplace, no book, no course could ever impart.

When his son was born, the world seemed to pause. Reginald was there. He was present there, holding the small, fragile body in his arms. The boy's tiny fingers curled innately around his own, and in that moment, Reginald felt both terrified and exalted. Nothing in his life had prepared him for the weight of that responsibility, for the sudden realization that another life now looked to him for protection, guidance, and love.

Those early years were a gift. He watched his son stumble into his first steps, his words tumbling from his mouth like roses and diamonds. He laughed at the mispronunciations, cheered at every little milestone. He was there to see scraped knees, to hear the shrieks of joy when his boy discovered the thrill of running. Those memories became like jewels in his heart; moments of pure, unfiltered fatherhood.

But time does not offer the same gifts twice. When his daughter was born nearly six years later, the story unfolded differently. By then, Reginald's life had already carried him away from home. Work demanded his presence in places far from the small circle of his family. And so, when his daughter entered the world, he was not there to hold her. He was absent in that first cry, absent in all the warm moments of a newborn's welcome.

He did not see her until she was already one month old. Even then, time was cruel. He could stay only two days before leaving again, duty pulling him toward a new chapter at the Plettenberg Bay Hotel. He kissed her tiny face, memorized the shape of her fingers, inhaled the newborn scent that every parent treasures, and then boarded a bus that took him farther away than miles could measure. The early days of her life, those sacred beginnings, were lost to him.

Her first birthday came, and again, he was not there. The candles were lit, the cake was cut, but her father was not among the hands that clapped and cheered. Reginald carried that absence like a wound. He did not get to hold her as a newborn, did not hear her first laughter in person, did not watch her teetering steps across the floor. Those moments slipped past him like waves against a ship, beautiful but untouchable.

And yet, love finds its way.

Though distance stood between them, a bond began to form in the most unlikely of ways. Technology became their bridge. Over the phone, he spoke to her daily, his voice traveling across time zones and oceans. She learned to recognize him not through touch or presence, but through sound. To her, "Daddy" was a voice on the line, a pixelated face glowing faintly on a video call. For almost two years, that was the only father she knew.

There were days when he worried that the bond would never be real, that he would always be a stranger whose face lived inside a phone screen. But children, with their innocence and resilience, have a way of teaching adults about what matters. She did not measure love by proximity. She measured it by consistency, by the fact that he was there, even if "there" meant through the crackling speaker of a call.

When he finally came home after years of this long-distance parenting, she was no longer the infant he had left behind. She was walking, talking, filled with a brightness that lit every room she entered. Reginald braced himself for her rejection, for the confusion of a child suddenly confronted with the physical presence of a man she had only known in images. Indeed, the first days were indeed difficult. She was shy, hesitant, almost frightened by the reality of him. For two days, she pulled away, hiding behind her mother, uncertain if she could trust what her eyes now saw.

Those two days were among the hardest of his life. He felt as though the absence of years had finally come to claim its debt. But love does not surrender easily. Reginald stayed soft, tried tediously, and made sure his presence was not faltered. Slowly, she reached out. A smile here, a curious glance there. Then one day, she climbed into his lap without hesitation, as if something inside her had decided: *Yes, this is my father.* From that moment, the bond was sealed.

Today, father and daughter are inseparable. Where he goes, she follows. Where she laughs, he joins. She brings him a joy that no absence can undo. The years of distance, the birthdays missed, the moments lost, all of it seems to dissolve in the warmth of the present they now share.

Reginald often reflects on the contrast between his two children. With his son, he was present, a witness to beginnings. With his daughter, he was absent, forced to love from afar until the distance narrowed. Yet, both relationships taught him the same truth: presence is not always measured in hours, but in intention. Children remember consistency more than they remember calendars.

Still, he cannot deny the ache. Each missed milestone weighs on him, especially when he thinks of his daughter's earliest days. The guilt sometimes creeps in during quiet moments aboard the cruise ship. He wonders how many more birthdays will pass without his presence, how many more times he will have to watch through a screen rather than from a seat at the table. But when the guilt threatens to consume him, he reminds himself of why he sacrifices. His absence, painful as it is, is woven into the effort of providing for them, of building a life that ensures their future.

There are moments, too, when fatherhood becomes his greatest source of strength. During long nights at sea, when the sounds from the engine and deck echo in the cabin, he thinks of them. He recalls his son's first steps, his daughter's hesitant smile when she finally reached for him. Those memories become his anchor, steadying him against loneliness, reminding him that love can span oceans.

His children do not yet understand the depth of what he carries—the sacrifices, the absences, the way he quietly places their dreams above his own. Perhaps one day they will. For now, they simply know him as Daddy: the man who calls, who listens, who cheers for their smallest victories, who returns home with stories of faraway seas. And perhaps, in the innocence of their love, that is enough.

Reginald often tells himself that life is rarely fair. It takes one hand and gives with the other. It robbed him of moments with his daughter, yet gave him the chance to rediscover her love in a way that felt almost miraculous. It blessed him with his son's early milestones, yet taught him through his daughter's distance that bonds are not broken by absence if they are rooted in love.

Now, as he sails across the world, he carries his children in his heart like guiding stars. They are the unseen companions of his journey, the reason behind his endurance, the meaning behind his sacrifices. For them, he can smile through pain, withstand loneliness, and face storms without fear.

***

When Reginald thought of his children side by side, the differences between them were unmistakable. They were of the same blood, born into the same family, yet they carried themselves into the world with such contrasting manners that it amazed him.

His son had taken his time, moving carefully through the milestones of childhood. Walking, talking—each came slowly, like a tree that grows not in a hurry but with deliberate patience. There was a gentleness in the way his boy unfolded into life, as if he had chosen to savor each stage before letting go of it. Reginald often smiled at the memory of coaxing those first words, of steadying those first wobbly steps. It had been a journey of waiting, of encouraging, of marveling at how even the slowest growth could feel like the most miraculous.

But his daughter... She was different. She arrived in the world as if racing against time. Before she was even a year and a half old, she was walking confidently, words spilling from her mouth with a speed that left even adults startled. Where his son had tread carefully, she leapt forward, eyes wide, mind sharp, spirit uncontainable. Hyperactive, quick to learn, quick to argue, she was a fire that burned bright in every room. Now, at five years old, she carried herself with a confidence that sometimes felt far beyond her age. She could reason like an adult, question things others might accept, and speak with a certainty that reminded Reginald of strong women he had known in his youth.

Perhaps that was why he chose her name carefully. He named her after his aunt, a woman from his father's side of the family who has embodied resilience and strength. Her name is Reotshepile Dorcars. Naming his daughter after her was not just a tribute; it was a wish, a blessing, a way of passing down a legacy. Every time he spoke her name, he felt the thread of history woven into the present, as if his aunt's spirit had found a way to live again in the child's determination and boldness.

Yet even with that legacy, he could not escape the ache of absence. His work pulled him far from home, and no matter how much he wanted to be there, time was not his to command. In a year, he managed barely two months with his daughter. Eight weeks scattered across twelve long months. The math was cruel, and he felt it every time he packed his bag to return to the ship. He wanted more; more days of laughter, more shared meals, more simple moments that fathers often take for granted. He felt the weight of what he owed her, a debt that could never be repaid with gifts or money, only with time.

Still, when he was home, her presence was undeniable. The house without her was a dead shell, a place where air seemed heavy with waiting. But the moment she returned from school, the walls themselves seemed to brighten. Joy rushed in with her laughter, and the silence dissolved into chatter, questions, and stories. She filled the rooms not just with sound but with life. Her energy became the life of the household, a reminder that childhood carries a magic no absence can fully extinguish.

She was particular too, in ways that amused and impressed him. For one so young, she already knew her mind. She had preferences, choices, even opinions about food that she defended with the determination of someone much older. If she did not want something, no amount of coaxing could change her. But if she decided on a thing, she embraced it fully, with the conviction of spirit that reminded Reginald again of the strong women of his family. She was decisive, firm, and utterly certain of who she was, even at five years old.

His son, quieter and more measured, balanced her fiery nature in the way siblings often do. They quarreled at times, but their bond was clear, their love for each other was evident in the way they protected each other. And both of them shared one trait that made Reginald laugh every time he thought of it: their love for milk.

Milk was their delight, their weakness, their simple joy. Whether it was cornmeal porridge, oats, or pap made from maize, they demanded it swimming in milk. He would sometimes sit back and watch them drink with a satisfaction so pure it seemed to belong only to children. The irony was not lost on him; he himself disliked milk, had never cared for it. But his children could not get enough. It became their trademark, their shared bond, the thing that tied them together in small, everyday rituals.

And so, he nicknamed them both his "Kit Cats." The name stuck, a term of endearment that captured their love for milk and their playful nature. Whenever he called them that, their faces lit up with delight, their laughter echoing through the house like bells. It was a small thing, a private family joke, but for Reginald it carried the weight of love. In those moments, he was not the man burdened by absence, not the worker trapped on a ship far from home. He was simply a father, smiling at the sight of his children, grateful for the joy they brought.

But beneath the laughter and the nicknames, the ache remained. Each year, he measured his time with them not in the number of days he was present, but in the milestones he missed. He thought of the school events he could not attend, the birthdays celebrated through screens, the moments when his daughter's sharp mind asked questions that deserved more than a rushed answer before work called him away again. He wondered what kind of memories they would carry of him when they were older. Would they remember the long absences, or would they remember the steady voice on the phone, the unwavering love that reached across oceans?

Reginald often prayed it would be the latter. He hoped that when they looked back, they would see not a father who was absent, but a father who gave everything he had for their sake. A father who loved them so fiercely that he endured loneliness, distance, and exhaustion so that they could have more.

The truth was, they were his anchor. On the ship, when the days blurred into endless routines and the nights grew heavy with solitude, it was thoughts of his children that carried him through. He remembered their laughter, their stubbornness, even their small quarrels, and he felt stronger. They gave meaning to the sacrifices, turning every hardship into something he could endure.

In their differences, he saw a portrait of life itself: slow and steady like his son, fast and fiery like his daughter. Both paths were valid, both beautiful, both necessary. Together, they reminded him that life unfolds in many ways, and that love is large enough to embrace them all.

The Kit Cats. His children. His legacy. His reason.

And among both of those reasons, Reginald often said that his daughter was a force of nature. Brilliant, energetic, and endlessly talkative, she seemed to embody the very spirit of curiosity itself. From the moment she woke until the moment she collapsed into sleep, words poured from her lips; questions, observations, little stories woven from the fabric of her young imagination. Her energy filled not only the rooms of their home but the corners of his heart, reminding him daily that life itself was a conversation waiting to be had.

And yet, it was not only her brightness that gave his life meaning. It was the way both of his children, in their differences and their similarities, stood as his greatest treasures. Together, they gave shape to his purpose. They were the reason he endured long months away from home, the reason he shouldered the relentless demands of shipboard life, the reason he pressed forward even when fatigue and loneliness weighed him down. In every smile, in every laugh, in every achievement of theirs, he saw proof that his sacrifices were not in vain.

His son was now standing at the threshold of adulthood, preparing to enter university. That thought filled Reginald with a mix of pride and disbelief. Had it not been only yesterday that he was coaxing his boy to take his first steps, steadying his small frame against the inevitable fall? Now the boy was a man, ready to take his own steps into the wider world. Reginald felt the tug of years, the swift passing of time that fathers always realize too late. But he also felt immense pride. His son's path was opening before him, and though Reginald could not always be there in person, he knew he had given him what mattered most: love, guidance, and the strength to carry himself with dignity.

His daughter, younger by years but no less vital to his heart, had her own long road ahead. She was only beginning her journey, her years still a canvas waiting to be painted. Yet Reginald already knew that she carried within her the tools to flourish. Her intelligence, her confidence, her spark, they would take her far, perhaps farther than even she could imagine. He smiled when he thought of it: the boy stepping into manhood, the girl racing through childhood with her fiery spirit. Different journeys, but bound together by the same foundation—his love.

Reginald loved them equally, deeply, without hesitation and without condition. That kind of love did not measure milestones, did not weigh absence against presence. It simply *was*. Unshakable, unchanging. Whether near or far, whether watching them in person or through the glow of a screen, his love remained the constant of their lives.

To have both a son and a daughter, he often thought, was to hold the fullness of life in one's hands. A blessing, a gift beyond measure. They were not just his children; they were his joy, his reason, his legacy, and his future. Everything he was, everything he strove to be, was tied to them. And as long as they thrived, he knew his story would always carry meaning.

Chapter 12: Moving Forward

There have been many thorns in the vast field of Reginald's struggles. He is smart enough to dodge many of them, yet too weak by innate human nature to keep some stabbed in his heart. These thorns are what we refer to as bad feelings. Sometimes, we are all smart enough to pay heed, listen to them, and work on them. Sometimes, these turn into bottled spells and always find the worst time to break out.

When he first arrived in Plettenberg, Reginald carried an excitement that could almost be touched. A new workplace, a new environment, new possibilities. He did not notice the thorns at first. He was too busy performing joy, too busy convincing the world and himself that he was whole again. He worked as though energy were infinite, as though discipline alone could erase pain. But the body has its own voice, and it cannot be silenced forever.

The silent voices in his head that he had been ignoring for so long finally roared one night at 2 a.m., when he stumbled half-awake to the bathroom and collapsed. The fall was sudden, merciless, his chin slamming against the bathtub. A sharp and unforgettable pain seared through him. He lay there, stunned with a realization that chilled him—this could have ended differently. This could have ended entirely. He could have collapsed and taken his last breath two seconds ago.

At the hospital, the words that came out of the doctor's mouth left Reginald staring into empty space: stress and depression. Two diagnoses wrapped in syllables that explained far more than they concealed. In that moment, the years of unpaid overtime, of swallowing frustrations, of silencing his own fatigue, rushed back like a tide. It all made sense. He had been carrying a storm inside, refusing to admit its weight, hoping the world would only notice the sunshine.

For the first time, he understood that depression was not about what the eye could see. It was about wounds buried deep, hidden in the folds of memory, carried in silence until the body itself rebelled. That night forced him to stop. To reframe. To reconsider the very structure of his life.

He began to learn to be gentle with himself. To admit that forgiveness, even forgiveness of past employers, of injustices endured, was not an eraser. Scars remained. They always do. What mattered was how one chose to reflect on them: with bitterness, or with an understanding that they shape the present.

Through self-introspection, he resolved not only to look inward but to find solutions. Many people, he realized, reflect endlessly without ever shifting. He did not want reflection to be his prison; he wanted it to be his key.

And so, he shifted. He made health a priority, both physical and mental. He sought balance in places where once he had only pursued achievement. He allowed himself to feel pain without being defined by it.

The lesson was not easy, but it was clear: true success is not applause from others. True success is the ability to confront your own wounds and still rise with strength and positivity. Pain does not vanish; it lingers, but it can become a strange kind of fuel. Like a tennis ball slammed against a wall, life will always rebound with force. The question is how you receive that rebound. Will you collapse? Or will you stand taller? For him, pain became courage.

In the silence that followed those depressed months, Reginald often thought of the barefoot boy who once ran across Pella's dusty ground, chasing whirlwinds and carrying buckets of rainwater. That boy had learned resilience early. And perhaps, without knowing it, he had always been preparing for this moment.

He also thought about the man in the mirror from years earlier. The one who once asked, "Who are you pretending to be?" That mirror had not lied. It had only asked him to reconcile both truths: the barefoot child and the man in polished shoes. Now, in his closing chapter, he saw them not as separate, but as one.

Every scar, every unanswered question, every door closed in his face had not erased him—they had refined him.

His career, though decorated with accolades, was never simply about wine or hospitality. It was about presence. About showing up, fully, in spaces where he was not always welcomed, and carving belonging where none had been offered. It was about dignity in greeting the cleaner before the CEO, refusing to eat alone if someone else was hungry, carrying his grandmother's teachings into boardrooms and wine cellars.

Plettenberg became more than a workplace. It became a mirror of his own transformation. Here, he learned not only how to serve others but also how to serve himself. To listen to his body. To trust his spirit. To forgive, but not forget. To take pain as preparation.

And so, as he looked back on his journey, he saw not a linear path but a series of echoes. The echo of his grandmother's voice, pointing knives at whirlwinds. The echo of his aunt's questions planted seeds of belief. The echo of city lights blinking on the horizon of a boyhood night. The echo of friends who drifted away, some into silence, some into shadows. The echo of laughter in dusty fields, of hunger that sharpened resolve, of moments that tried to break him but only built him.

The echoes never faded. They guided him towards a new direction.

Now, in the twilight of his professional life, Reginald did not measure success in titles or salaries. He measured it in resilience. In the ability to rise after collapse. In the courage to remain kind when bitterness would have been easier. In the stubborn choice to keep believing even when the world tried to teach him otherwise.

He often returned, in memory, to the boy at the edge of Pella, staring at distant lights and whispering to the sky. That boy had asked for more, not knowing how or when it would arrive. And here he was, an answer to his own childhood prayer. Not perfect. Not without scars. But alive, present, and unbroken.

The journey had been long. The cost had been high. But the reward was simple: to stand here now, whole, and say, *I am still here.*

He was no longer pretending. He was becoming. And becoming was enough.

And perhaps that was the truest success of all.

Education had always been both a challenge and a treasure for Reginald. He did not walk the well-paved road many of his peers followed, the one that led directly to university, libraries, and framed degrees. Instead, his path bent quickly toward work. At first, that felt like a detour, a mark of what he had missed. But over the years, he realized it was not a detour at all. It was a different curriculum, an education in real time, paid for with sweat, persistence, and humility.

Managers became his lecturers. Colleagues became classmates. Mistakes became examinations he could not avoid. From them, he learned things no textbook had spelled out. He absorbed the language of accounting while balancing ledgers late into the night, the nuances of management through watching both good leaders and poor ones, and the subtle dance of human relationships from the countless moments where silence taught more than words.

There were times he sat across tables with men and women carrying PhDs, their qualifications stitched neatly after their names. He had none. What he carried instead was curiosity and honesty, sharpened by necessity. Where he lacked formal credentials, he asked questions. Where he felt unprepared, he leaned into the courage of admitting what he did not know. That simple courage—the ability to say, *teach me*—turned strangers into mentors and obstacles into opportunities.

In time, he came to see that education is not a singular event but a lifelong unfolding. It is not defined solely by buildings and certificates, but by a person's willingness to keep learning, to remain open, to stay hungry.

Still, formal education remained a key he had not fully unlocked. He had begun courses here and there, some abandoned midway, some carried further, but never in the tidy, uninterrupted arc he once imagined for himself. Earlier in his journey, those unfinished courses had felt like failures. Regret gnawed at him, whispering that he had left something incomplete. But with age and reflection, he released that weight. Not all things are meant to be corrected. Some remain as reminders, not burdens.

"I no longer dwell on regret," he would tell himself. "Some things I can fix, others I must forgive." That truth set him free to move forward without shame.

One of his deepest motivations in continuing to learn was personal: his son. In the quiet of evenings, father and child would talk not only about schoolwork but about systems—the invisible forces that shape how people grow, stumble, and rise. Reginald spoke of education, yes, but also of habits. Of character. Of the choices made when no one was watching.

He reminded his son that a degree, while valuable, is not the final measure of a person. What endures are the values you live by, the habits you nurture, and the consistency with which you pursue what matters. A certificate may open a door, but it cannot guarantee respect. Respect is earned in how you show up, how you treat people, how you keep promises.

These were lessons Reginald carried from his own background. Though humble and often hard, his beginnings were a foundation he could not despise. They had carved in him a hunger to learn, a refusal to remain still, and an unshakable pride in resilience. Even in the most difficult days, the echo of his school motto whispered like a guide: *Shun mediocrity and embrace excellence.* Those words had been simple on paper, but they became scripture in his daily walk.

Figures from afar also fueled his fire. He often reflected on the story of Jack Ma, the Chinese entrepreneur who faced rejection after rejection—applications declined, opportunities withheld, paths blocked. Yet through resilience and an almost stubborn belief in himself, Ma rose. It wasn't the billions that inspired Reginald, but the persistence. The testimony that background does not decide destiny.

Such stories mirrored his own belief: that excellence grows not from ease but from endurance.

Looking back, Reginald could trace the long arc of his life—from the barefoot boy in Pella, to the young man wrestling with city lights and language barriers, to the professional who stood in polished shoes yet never forgot the soil beneath them. The arc was not smooth. It was marked with fractures, doubts, and detours. But those breaks became the very proof of resilience.

Success, he had learned, does not erase wounds. It does not wipe the slate clean or silence the echoes of hunger, shame, or exclusion. What success offers instead is a chance to live with those wounds differently, to wear them as part of your story, to let them teach rather than torment, to allow them to become a light for someone else still struggling in the dark.

His journey, then, was not about perfection. It was about acceptance. About forgiving himself for the roads not taken, the studies left unfinished, the silences that sometimes lingered too long. It was about determination, an unrelenting hunger to improve, to lift not just himself but those around him.

Every step he took was a way of carrying his story proudly, not as a secret but as a lantern. He knew that by sharing it, others might see their own strength reflected. Others might recognize that pain does not mean failure, that wounds do not disqualify, that beginnings in dust can still lead to corridors of glass and timber.

To Reginald, this was the legacy worth leaving: not the title before his name or the signature beneath it, but the testimony that resilience is possible, and that even in the midst of hardship, one can choose excellence.

And so, as he approached the final chapters of his career, he did not think of endings but of continuations. The boy from Pella still walked with him. The man in the mirror still watched him. His son still listened. And the world, forever in its constant orbit, still needed his story.

That was enough. More than enough.

www.ingramcontent.com/pod-product-compliance
Lightning Source LLC
Chambersburg PA
CBHW051627140626
46547CB00033B/2725